This is an unprecedented time in history and a pivotal moment for you and your family. Now more than ever we need to learn how to attract and host the presence of God. *Creating a Habitation for God's Glory* by Pastor Todd Smith is your difference maker!

SID ROTH, Host
It's Supernatural! Television

CREATING A HABITATION FOR

GOD'S GLORY

BECOMING A RESTING PLACE FOR THE POWER AND
PRESENCE OF THE HOLY SPIRIT

TODD SMITH

DESTINY IMAGE® PUBLISHERS, INC.

P.O. Box 310, Shippensburg, PA 17257-0310

"Promoting *Inspired Lives.*"

This book and all other Destiny Image and Destiny Image Fiction books are available at Christian bookstores and distributors worldwide.

Cover design by Eileen Rockwell

Interior designed by Terry Clifton

For more information on foreign distributors, call 717-532-3040.

Reach us on the Internet: www.destinyimage.com.

ISBN 13 TP: 978-0-7684-5408-6

ISBN 13 eBook: 978-0-7684-5409-3

ISBN 13 HC: 978-0-7684-5411-6

ISBN 13 LP: 978-0-7684-5410-9

For Worldwide Distribution, Printed in the U.S.A.

2 3 4 5 6 7 8 / 24 23 22 21

DEDICATION

The Lord spoke to me, "The fate of the nation (USA) is in the hands of the Church." My prayer is that the men and women standing behind the pulpits of our churches would grasp the gravity of this hour. More than ever we need leaders who know how to attract and host the presence and glory of God. I enthusiastically dedicate this book to all the faithful pastors who are leading us into the greatest move of God the world has ever seen.

ACKNOWLEDGMENTS

Special thanks to my wife, Karen. You have never stopped encouraging me to keep pressing onward. Your constant support has propelled me to start and finish this book. Your pursuit of the Word of God and its Author, at times has left me speechless. Your love for me and our boys is the backbone of our family. Thanks for always seeing the positive in all things.

I also want to express my deep love and appreciation to the people I get to do life with every day—the executive and support staff at Christ Fellowship Church. I am thankful for the integrity, passion, and hunger you have for the Lord and His work. Only history will reveal the full impact your lives and ministries are having on this generation. You have been chosen for this moment.

CONTENTS

Part One

FROM
DESPERATION
TO REVIVAL

METEORITES AND FIREWATER

"A revived church is the only hope for a dying world."

—ANDREW MURRAY

On Monday December 10, 1984, at approximately 5:30 in the afternoon, a small, quiet southern town was hit by a 3-pound meteorite traveling more than 300 mph. The extra-terrestrial rock fell out of the sky and struck the metal mailbox belonging to Mr. and Mrs. Carutha Barnard in Claxton, Georgia, a town best known for its adventurous rattlesnake round-ups and also known the world over for its fruitcake. In fact, it has been unof-ficially tagged "The Fruitcake Capital of the World." However, everything changed on this otherwise uneventful day when the sky rock plummeted into the town and hit the infamous mail-box. Why "infamous mailbox"? Years later a meteorite collector paid $83,000 for that broken mail receptor. Thus named the most expensive mailbox in the world.[1]

Also in Georgia there is another small, quiet town of about 3,100 residents, Dawsonville, where I pastor Christ Fellowship Church. Dawsonville is approximately fifty miles northeast of Atlanta. We are famous for three things: 1) NASCAR racing; 2) Georgia's tallest waterfall, Amicalola Falls; and 3) moonshine. Each year in October our quaint hometown hosts more than 100,000 people attending the Mountain Moonshine Festival.

I do believe the Lord has a sense of humor, here's why. Society has multiple names for illicitly distilled liquor including: moon-shine; white lightning; hooch; mash liquor; homebrew; mountain dew; and my favorite, firewater. I find it funny that God chose to visit Dawsonville—host to an international moonshine festival—and give new meaning to the word "firewater"!

ENDNOTE

1. http://www.northwestgeorgianews.com/georgia-mailbox-hit-by-meteorite-sells-for-bizarre-new/article_cc65f716-cc01-5967-bbc6-8c44dc47c14a.html; accessed May 15, 2020.

2

HE STEPPED INTO
THE ROOM

"The first thing most churches need to do is get God to attend."
—STEVE GRAY

I wasn't scheduled to be in the classroom that night, but Karen, my wife, chancellor of the KINEO Ministry Training Center invited me to address her students. For several weeks she had been teaching about the past: "Revivals and Revivalists." She highlighted how these moves of God in the past transformed entire communities, regions, and nations. For example, the Welsh Revival, Azusa Street, the Awakenings, Hebrides Revival, etc., were all mentioned and discussed.

My assignment was clear; I was to share about our experiences with revival and particularly the Pensacola Outpouring at Brownsville Assembly of God in Pensacola, Florida. Even though I was thrilled about communicating my experience, I intended to be in the classroom no more than fifteen minutes.

As Karen and I addressed the class and responded to questions, it became apparent the students' thirst and hunger for God was extremely high. The discussion wasn't surface oriented or a casual curiosity; no, there was a depth to it. A desperation and longing for Him was everywhere. Collectively, the students wanted to know why couldn't He do it again, right now and right here at our church?

The more we talked, the more their hunger intensified.

Then it happened. God stepped into the room. I know that seems like an unusual statement, but He came. He didn't announce His arrival; He softly entered the classroom and walked among us.

We all knew something just occurred, the atmosphere changed; the dynamics of the room in an instant shifted. It was a moment none of us will ever forget. The twenty-five students pushed their chairs away from the table and each fell to the floor—some to their knees, some flat on the floor—with their faces bowed. Karen and I joined them. Many cried out for mercy, some worshipped, while others just wept. I could hear them sobbing, wailing, and openly repenting. The more we repented, the more He manifested.

The moment was heavenly and otherworldly. Jesus walked among us. He was tenderly yet fervently revealing Himself to the group—yet to each of us individually at the same time. It was holy, no one moved or drew attention to themselves. We were in a moment that not many people get to experience. I committed to do whatever necessary to experience Him again.

Nothing Happened for a Year

Can you imagine what I was thinking? Because of that experience, I expected our church to be in a season of growth and revival. I just knew God was going to visit us the following Sunday morning the same way He visited us in the classroom. My faith was soaring and my joy was through the roof. Guess what? The following Sunday was less than spectacular; it was just a normal Sunday. Honestly, it was as if what took place in the classroom never happened. To say I was disappointed, discouraged, and frustrated is putting it mildly. I truly expected God to do on Sunday morning what He did at KINEO Ministry Training Center.

Days, weeks, months, and an entire year came and went and we never encountered Him in that way again. Don't get me wrong, we were having good church, lives were being changed and folks were developing in their faith, but nothing like what happened on that evening when He stepped in the room. The heavens seemed closed for a solid year.

Why the delay?

God Tested the Water

Scriptures reveal that before God invaded a land or city He typically sent a contingent ahead in order to determine strengths, weaknesses, and overall tendencies of the people. For example, before the children of Israel were to take possession of the Promised Land, He instructed Moses to send twelve of his men to spy out the land. God wanted these men to not only measure the nation's military power, economic strengths and weaknesses, but also any structural vulnerabilities. In addition, they were to observe the inhabitants of the land and inspect and sample the agricultural capacity. In other words, what was the nation able to produce and protect. According to Numbers 13, these twelve walked to and fro making observations of the inhabitants. When they returned, they reported to Moses all they discovered.

Also, as another example, Joshua sent spies to take an inside look at Jericho before they conquered it.

Jesus surveilled a situation in advance as well. You may know the story of Jesus turning over the tables in the temple (Matthew 21:12). This wasn't a spontaneous release of frustration, no. Jesus visited the day before and took a look around the temple to see all the activities taking place inside His house.

> And Jesus went into Jerusalem and into the temple. So **when He had looked around at all things**, as the hour was already late, He went out to Bethany with the twelve (Mark 11:11).

This is what God does before He inhabits a church. He will come in and spy the land. He will take a look around, investigate, observe, and determine if the church has the capacity to carry His glory and host His presence. He will come in and measure its strength (see Zechariah 2).

I believe this is exactly what God did to us that day when He visited the classroom. He came and took a look around.

This not only applies to us, but every church. You see, before God's manifest presence resides perpetually in a church or ministry, He will visit and take a close look. So what exactly was He doing in our classroom? I am convinced there were three aspects of our church that God wanted to know: 1) the environment; 2) our temperature; 3) our capacity. Let's take a closer look at each of these three:

1. God Was Evaluating the Environment

Environments matter, especially in churches. Not every church has the right environment to be able to host Him long term. Visitation yes, long term no. God wanted to know if our church had the right environment.

2. God Took Our Temperature

He came in and took a census of how we would we respond to His activity. He was looking closely at how we would react to His interruption. Would we push forward with our agenda or surrender to His. Would we fall forward or backward? Would we make the encounter about us or Him? Would we repent and honor Him or would we cry out for blessings?

3. God Measured Our Capacity

What level of hunger did this group of leaders actually have— was it superficial or genuine? Could they hold up under the weight of glory that was to come? What weight limit did they have?

God does this to ministries, churches, and people all the time. He takes the temperature of the church, evaluates its environment, and measures its capacity to host Him.

When He walked into that unassuming classroom, I had no idea it would be fifty-one weeks later before I had a similar encounter. In the meantime, Heaven seemed to be shut up over my life and church. I often questioned what I had done that obviously offended Him. In my opinion there must have been something in me that kept Him away. Needless to say the enemy capitalized on my interpretation of the silence.

3

I DECIDED TO QUIT

"Revival brings back a holy shock to apathy and carelessness."
—WINKIE PRATNEY

I didn't quite understand after God's visit in the classroom why we didn't experience immediate revival and growth to our church. So, out of desperation and exasperation I called the church into a 21-day fast in January 2018. I typically stayed away from the "first of the year" type fasts because I felt they had become too "commercialized," but I longed for a fresh outpouring of His Spirit.

Here is what was truly happening in my heart before and during our fast. We had a visitation of God in the classroom, but nothing since that time. So I was deeply discouraged, yet hopefully desiring a move of God. I was entering my eighth year of ministry at Christ Fellowship and we were stagnant. It was a beautiful church family, but we were stuck. I felt fully responsible for the ineffectiveness of our church.

The devil played with my mind. He would whisper to me, "You are the reason God hasn't blessed this church. If you were any good, they would come. These people don't love you. The people leave the church because of you." In the middle of my sermon his voice would speak to me, "They are never gonna get it. You're wasting your time. Someone else could do a better job."

The harassment wasn't limited to when I was at the church. Oh no, satan would capitalize most often on my ride home from church after the Sunday morning service. He would shout in my ear, "Your crowd was small today. People are leaving the church and you are the reason. You are a weak leader."

The enemy's assaults were relentless and the constant barrage of indictments were brutal. The attacks were having an immense toll on me, especially emotionally.

The fast started out normally; however, just over two weeks into the fast something happened I will never forget. Let me explain. Each day I would make my way into the sanctuary to pray; then one morning as I was walking across the platform toward our baptistery, out of nowhere I had an open vision.

In the natural, the baptistery was empty, there was no water in the tank. However, in the vision I saw the baptistery full of water and there was fire on the surface of the water. The fire on the water was two to three feet wide and stretched from the front of the baptistery to the back. It reminded me how gasoline burns on top of water. The open vision lasted a short eight to ten seconds.

As soon as the vision ended, the Lord spoke clearly to me, I will never forget what He said, "I am going to baptize people with Holy Spirit fire."

This one vision has shaped my life and calling and is having a global impact, as well. Thousands of people have come from all around the world to encounter the fire of God in the baptismal waters at Christ Fellowship Church in Dawsonville, Georgia.

Just a few weeks after the heavenly vision, the glory of God sat down in our sanctuary. Thousands of lives have encountered it. My desire is to host Him well and create an atmosphere both individually and corporately that He is attracted to. My passion and pursuit is to be a resting place for the power and presence of the Holy Spirit.

This book reveals our journey and shares insights how you can encounter His power and presence as well.

MY DARK ROOM EXPERIENCE

4

Friday is usually a "date day" for Karen, my wife, and me. However, this particular Friday was unlike any other. A week had passed since the vision the Lord gave me of the baptistery. I knew the Lord spoke to me regarding the fire on the water, but I didn't understand the full depth of the vision. I woke up and immediately felt a heaviness, and I was extremely frustrated and depressed. I sluggishly rolled out of bed and walked into the living room; I didn't even bother to turn on any lights.

Karen knew something was wrong and rightfully discerned that I needed some time by myself to work through whatever was bothering me.

While sitting on the brown swivel stool at the counter in our kitchen, I methodically started evaluating my ministry. Once again my mind immediately drifted to all the things that weren't right about me and the church. The more I thought about my ministry and the church, the more distraught I became.

I felt incapable, unqualified, and ineffective as the lead pastor. The full weight of ministry failures had a voice and they shouted in my ear. Every failure was exposed and every flaw was magnified. After a couple of hours of this mental and spiritual torture, I succumbed to the pressure. I lifted my hands above my head and shouted to the Lord, "I'm done, I quit! I can't do this anymore! Someone else can have it!"

I wished I could say a sense of God's reassuring love and presence rushed over me, but it didn't. Everything went quiet. I didn't feel anything. It was eerily tranquil in a way. The silence shocked me. I expected some type of protest or hooray, something, but I got nothing. I think both Heaven and hell were caught off guard, somewhat surprised. It may have been that both kingdoms got what they wanted.

However, the silence only substantiated my feelings that God was unconcerned, unmoved—or was in full agreement with my decision.

After my "dark room" experience on Friday, I had to preach on Sunday. Even in the midst of my struggle, God spoke to me about the word I was to preach to my people. I arrived at church early and very hopeful. I had a wonderfully timed sermon about the necessity of laying down our lives on the altar and dying to ourselves. I knew the message was from God.

The worship segment of the service was moving, something was happening in the sanctuary. As I stood behind the pulpit, I strongly sensed the presence of God on me. I preached with confidence and boldness. I gave everything I had. I pleaded with the people to lay down their lives and serve Him. However, throughout the message the people were expressionless, they just stared at me. It seemed as if they were bored. I interpreted their response as rejection, which only added to my growing list of grievances and disappointments in myself.

After the service I didn't want to talk to anyone, so I quickly made my way to the car. I sat in the car hopeless. With my head tilted down, I wept; I was at the end of myself and I couldn't take it anymore. I raised my hands to God and told Him that I was doing all I knew to do, I was trying my very best, and there was no response from the people, no fire, zero.

I also took the opportunity to remind God of my fast, no food, and how I was preaching the whole counsel of the Bible. Again, Heaven was silent, not a single sound of encouragement or morsel of comfort. It was as if God wanted me to quit, die, or both. Honestly, I felt isolated and abandoned by the Lord. His silence further solidified my assumption that God was done with me at Christ Fellowship Church.

The Phone Call

In 2010 a friend invited me to attend a special service that a well-established prophet was having at his church. I reluctantly agreed and attended the meeting.

The woman prophet preached a great message and then the ministry time began—this is when things got interesting. I watched closely as she began to randomly call people out and prophesy over them. She came toward me and needless to say I was a bit nervous. I had no idea what she was going to say, but she had a word for me. She said, "A man from Texas will change your life forever."

Immediately, my mind started thinking, *Who do we know in Texas?* I couldn't think of a single person.

Karen and I often wondered who that man would be. The next few years we meet several men from Texas who loved and helped us, but we were not fully sure if they were the fulfillment of the prophetic word given to me on that day.

Every Tuesday we have a church staff meeting. However, this Tuesday's meeting followed my Friday encounter and also the horrific Sunday I mentioned earlier.

I arrived early and was waiting in the conference room for my staff to arrive—and still heavily discouraged from the weekend's experiences. One by one they entered the room and sat down like they have done for eight years, but this day was different. I didn't hesitate; I started the meeting by sharing my disappointment in where the church was on all fronts—numerically, financially, and spiritually. I acknowledged my fears and frustrations and took the full responsibility for being unable to take the church to the next level.

The staff were shocked when I told them that I was finished and that I was resigning my position as pastor. I said I would stay at the church until God opened another opportunity for me to pastor somewhere else. My wife was sitting to my right and could not believe what she heard. Karen's mouth opened in disbelief. She knew I was struggling but had no idea that I had reached this point.

Then the Unexpected Happened

A few days later, Marty Darracott, who at the time was our associate pastor as well as our youth pastor, received a phone call from Pat Schatzline. Pat is a well-known, highly effective international evangelist. I had never met Pat but Pastor Marty knew him.

The phone conversation Pat had with Marty was brief and to the point: "Marty, I had a dream this morning and I believe it was from the Lord. I saw a man in a dark room, no lights on, and he had his hands up in the air and he was very frustrated and he was saying, 'God, I can't do this anymore, I quit.'" Pat said, "Marty, I think the Lord was showing me your pastor."

The phone call so startled Pastor Marty that he hung up the phone without saying goodbye. He couldn't believe what he was hearing—it was exactly what I experienced on Friday and told my staff on Tuesday. Pat called back and Pastor Marty hurriedly asked Pat if he would tell me and Karen what the Lord showed him. He agreed.

Pastor Marty found Karen and then together they walked into the conference room where I was studying. Marty said, "Pastor, I think you need to hear this." He told us evangelist Pat Schatzline was on the phone and that the Lord spoke to him about me. Obviously, I was curious about what the Lord had said to Pat, because it seemed that I couldn't get the Lord to speak to me directly.

Pastor Marty put the phone on speaker and laid it down on the conference room table. Pat began to share what the Lord showed him, describing my Friday experience with uncanny accuracy. He said, "Todd, I had a dream this morning and I believe it was from the Lord. I saw a man in a dark room, no lights on, and he had his hands up in the air and he was very frustrated and he was saying, 'God, I can't do this anymore, I quit.'"

Again, he perfectly described my experience on Friday and at no time in my life have I ever had someone speak to me in this manner. It was as if he was in my house and heard my conversation with God. I knew I was receiving a direct word from God; and the more he spoke, the more emotional I became. I was amazed!

As Pat continued to tell me what the Lord revealed to him, the more the Lord settled into the room—the very room where I announced my resignation. Then Pat added, "And the Lord says, DON'T QUIT!"

After the call ended, we all just looked at each other. An overwhelming sense of relief flooded my mind. I was grateful and overwhelmed by the experience. Through all the ups and downs of my ministry at Christ Fellowship, I never doubted God's love for me; however, I just didn't think He knew where I was. This changed everything.

Needless to say, I immediately pulled back the resignation. My heart was filled with a new energy and hope. I didn't know what was going to happen next, but I believed that God knew where I was and that He didn't want me to quit! That's all I needed.

Guess what? Pat lives in Texas—and His word has changed my life forever!

5

THE IN-LAWS
ARE COMING

*"Sunday morning Christianity is the
greatest hindrance to true revival."*
—Vance Havner

I came across this gem of a quote from an article, "The
Relatives Are Coming!" in the *Los Angeles Times*—enjoy:
"Having in-laws stay over is like an Olympic competition. A great
deal of preparation is required to attempt to execute a flawless performance, and through it all you pray for good marks from the
judges—your in-laws. I wish I only had to endure this grueling
event every four years."[1]

That's cruel, but hilarious. I love it.

Now I must say I have the best mother-in-law in the world. She is a prize and is perfect in every way. And we all know that having a guest over for the weekend can be exhilarating, but it also can stressful and hectic to say the least. Someone's presence is an intrusion into our daily routine and puts everything to the test; it stretches us. We enjoy the conversation, fun, and interaction; nonetheless, it is an interruption in our predictably comfortable lives.

Make the Room Ready!

There is a gigantic difference in how you prepare the house and/or make a room ready for a short-term guest versus an extended-stay resident.

For weekend guests, we have two goals in the back of our minds: 1) give our special guests the best experience possible; 2) make just enough temporary adjustments in order to get through the weekend.

Knowing they are going to be with us for a short period, we put our best foot forward because we want their experience to be memorable and pleasant. The furniture is rearranged, we dust, vacuum, stock the pantry, and certainly make sure there is clean bedding, adequate bath towels, and plenty of toilet paper.

In addition, we remove as much of the collected clutter as possible and hide the stuff we don't want our guests to see. We strategically place those items in temporary holding zones, like under the bed, in closets, attic, and cabinets. Our thought, *It's only a short visit, will be over in a couple of days, and then we can get back to normal and carry on as usual.*

Before the guests arrive there are some unwritten rules that instinctively both the guests and hosts know. For example, guests don't have access to every room of the house. It's like a universal code—if the door is closed, it's off-limits, a no-go. Not overtly, but clandestine like. Permission is needed to enter such rooms. Why? There are areas that we know we need to clean up, but just haven't gotten around to it, and we don't want the guests to see the mess.

For long-term guests, however, our preparation is entirely different. Cordial extended stays don't just happen; in fact, it takes a great deal of effort on the part of the hosts to adequately prepare for extended stays. But a good host makes all the necessary adjustments to accommodate the new person, their needs and schedule. You have a new reality and must address questions such as: How best can we serve our guests? How will we work them into our daily activities? Interestingly, some of those adjustments are more drastic than others.

Often people treat Jesus as a weekend guest. They love Him, but only give Him access to particular rooms of their heart and life. Some of the areas in their lives are under their control, no-go zones, off-limit areas. The places where they hide all the clutter and stuff they accumulated over the years.

Are they saved? Yes. Will they go to Heaven when they die? Certainly; they are living in the grace of God. But are they carrying and operating in His glory? No. Here's why. God demands that our lives be consecrated to Him. He wants and must have access and dominion over every facet of our lives. He cannot place His glory on someone who is not totally and completely surrendered.

This is why many believers do not carry the glory of God and do not live operating in His manifest power.

Controlled Visitation Versus Uncontrolled Habitation

Over the years I have learned it is easy to receive, walk in, and carry the *grace* of God. It is a gift, freely given to those who ask for it. However, it is entirely different to receive, walk in, and carry the *glory* of God.

This is the same for churches. Most churches have the culture for a visit from the Lord rather than an all-invasive habitation.

The following true story is the difference you can expect when you go from a controlled visitation to uncontrolled habitation.

Blair was ten years old and completely deaf in her left ear. While in her first year of elementary school, a simple ear infection was misdiagnosed. The result was irreversible damage, her nerve endings were dead. The rest of her life she would be unable to hear out of her left ear; medically there was nothing they could do for her. In fact, not even a hearing aid or surgery could reverse her condition.

Blaire heard what Jesus was doing in the baptismal waters at our North Georgia Revival. She wanted to come and get baptized, believing that God could heal her. A few Sundays before she came, she was at home watching the revival on her computer. A particular woman caught her attention when she testified that she came to the revival, was baptized, and the Lord healed her of stage-four cancer. After hearing this testimony, Blair knew she needed to get baptized at the revival.

It was week eighty of the North Georgia Revival. While in the water, Blair made a bold statement that changed the whole atmosphere of the room, "If God can heal a lady with stage-four lung cancer, then God can heal me." It was a bold proclamation that resounded around the world. She had no doubt God would heal her deaf ear 100 percent. Pastor Marty Darracott saw her faith and began praying for her left ear to open. He placed his finger over her good ear so she could not hear the words he was speaking. Within seconds, her left ear was completely healed and to this day she has 100 percent hearing in the once-deaf ear.

We had virtually no miracles in our church prior to the habitation of the glory of God in our building. Now it is common, and unusual when healings don't take place. Thankfully our church decided we wanted total habitation rather than weekend visits from the Lord.

ENDNOTE

1. Wendy Vallier quoted by Julie Bawden Davis, in "The Relatives Are Coming!" Los Angeles Times, August 3, 1993; https://www.latimes.com/archives/la-xpm-1993-08-03-vw-19688-story.html; accessed May 16, 2020.

6

I LOST THE FACE OF GOD

"The depth of our repentance will determine the depth of our revival."
—FRANK BARTLEMAN

Years ago a small group of young families from our church spent July 4th at Stone Mountain Park in Stone Mountain, Georgia. The evening was delightful with lots of food and laughter and relaxing with friends. The highlight of the night was to be a world-class laser and fireworks show.

Our boys, at the time, were 10 and 8 years old. They were having the time of their lives playing and running around with their friends at this iconic state park. The laser and fireworks display brought closure to the evening. Immediately after being entertained by the explosions in the sky, we quickly gathered our things. I had Ty, our oldest, but quickly realized, no Ethan. I assumed Karen had him and she did the same of me. Our assumptions were wrong. There were thousands of people present and the park was dimly lit, virtually dark. Not only was it difficult to move around due to the large crowd, but we could barely see.

Word quickly spread to our group that Ethan was lost. Instantly, as you could imagine, our emotions were everywhere; we panicked. Our thoughts immediately raced to the worst-case scenario, all the while praying we would find him. We were racing through the crowd shouting his name. Karen went one way and I went the other way. Everyone with us joined the search. After about five minutes one of our friends located him. Ethan was crying. We were crying. We were all a mess of emotions. The reunion was sweet—so thankful and delighted he was safe.

Parents know the utter helplessness when a child is lost in a crowd. It is a horrific feeling.

Have you ever been lost? It's a terrible experience. I don't know which is worse, being lost or being the one responsible for keeping a child from becoming lost.

Jesus' parents know that utter helplessness feeling. Jesus was lost for three days; they had no idea where He was. Like us, Mary thought Jesus was with Joseph, and Joseph assumed the twelve-year-old was with His mom.

Would you believe me if I told you that I lost God? More specifically, the face of God? I know that may be a bizarre statement but it's true; let me explain how it happened.

I have had the honor to have pastored some amazing churches and witnessed some remarkable moves of the Spirit. When I became pastor of Christ Fellowship, I worked hard on growing and increasing our church at every level. Countless hours and meetings were invested in developing the church. Deep in my heart I wanted to see people saved, and for the new converts to walk out their new faith with consistency and passion. Throughout the years we had a lot of ups and downs. There were times of numeric growth and times of decline. In the midst of it all, I loved Him the best I knew how.

I fasted and prayed often that He would help me pastor and grow my wonderful church. I desperately wanted to see my people mature in their faith and not only love Him, but love Him well. However, in the midst of pastoring, counseling, studying for sermons, leading, preaching, praying, parenting, and living, I sadly lost His face. Somehow my attention and focus shifted from the *face* of God to the *things* of God. Honestly, it was unintentional, it just happened. What was most tragic is that I didn't even know it took place—it was a slow fade. I found myself more acquainted with His hand than His face.

You ask, how is that possible? It is very possible. Looking back at my experience, at some point in my relationship with Jesus it became mostly about me, my life, my destiny, needs and desires. Frankly, my prayer time was usually spent going over my lengthy list of things I wanted and needed God to do for me. And usually bringing back to His attention—complaining about— something He needed to do and hadn't done yet. The majority of our conversations were one sided, and you can guess who did most of the talking.

In December 2017, prior to our 21-day fast, I read Psalm 27. I camped out here for several days if not weeks, and my eyes were glued to verses 4 and 8. Every day I read these Scriptures:

> *One thing I have desired of the Lord, that will I seek: that I may dwell in the house of the Lord all the days of my life, to behold the beauty of the Lord, and to inquire in His temple* (Psalm 27:4).

> *When You said, "Seek My face," my heart said to You, "Your face, Lord, I will seek"* (Psalm 27:8).

Wow, verse 8! I never knew seventeen words could radically change a person's life—these did. The full weight of these words fell on my heart and it slowly crushed me. I felt as if God was speaking directly to me, for I was guilty of the same thing David the psalmist had done. Somewhere during my walk with God, perhaps while praying, ministering, preaching, and living life, like David I lost God's face.

What caused it? How did it happen? At some point in David's fantastic journey to the throne of Israel, his eyes shifted from the face of God to God's hands. Perhaps it was the constant need for protection from the pressure of his enemies, or the accolades and adoration he was receiving from his growing army. Whatever the cause, David drifted from the face of God. What is most alarming, David didn't even know he had lost His Father's face.

This worshipful psalm reveals the tender side of our heavenly Father who simply wanted His son to recapture His heart and face. God reached down and tugged on David's heart, God called a time-out. He pressed the pause button and said, in essence, "David, hey David, I am over here. Come and again seek My face." If God said this to David, the one whom He said, "David is a man after my own heart," how much more would it be necessary for me? If David could lose God's face, so could I—and I did.

I lost God's face the same way I lost Ethan. It happened in such a way that I didn't know it until I went looking for Him.

My prayer is that we would evaluate our walk with God. May we be honest and ask the Lord to search us and reveal where we are with Him. Let me encourage you to kneel before Him and ask for nothing but to simply behold His face. Then, watch what happens to your heart and walk with Him.

The following are a few passages that encourage us to seek His face:

2 Chronicles 7:14: *"if My people who are called by My name will humble themselves, and pray and seek My face, and turn from their wicked ways, then I will hear from heaven, and will forgive their sin and heal their land."*

Jeremiah 29:13-14: *"And you will seek Me and find Me, when you search for Me with all your heart. I will be found by you, says the Lord...."*

Psalm 63:1: *"O God, You are my God; early will I seek You; my soul thirsts for You; my flesh longs for You in a dry and thirsty land where there is no water."*

Psalm 105:4: *"Seek the Lord and His strength; seek His face evermore!"*

Psalm 27:8: *"When You said, 'Seek My face,' my heart said to You, 'Your face, Lord, I will seek.'"*

7

A LEAKY ROOF AND A PASTOR I DESPISED

"We will not have the fullness of the Spirit's outpouring until baptized people separate themselves completely from the world."
—DAVID WILKERSON

His name is Don Allen and he pastors a thriving church, The Church at War Hill. I didn't like him very much, probably not at all. In fairness, I probably wasn't his favorite either.

Over the years he and I had a few but serious issues with one another. I loved him in the Spirit because I had to, but my flesh didn't care for him. To make matters worse, our churches are only three and half miles apart. Naturally, because our churches are so close, there was a built-in competition—and it was obvious.

Things reached a boiling point and I asked Don to come by my office for a pastoral conversation. This was the appointed day I was going to unleash my built-up frustration because I felt he had stepped over the line on a couple of significant matters regarding a few of my people.

After entering my office and the cordial exchange of professional "niceties," I immediately went over my well-documented grievances. We locked horns and went at it. The meeting was professional but confrontational. At one point one of my staff members peaked in through my office door window to make sure we weren't killing each other.

I was blunt and firm, and in return he was just as candid. At one point I called him a "rattlesnake." Yep, I called him a serpent. I likened him to satan; I was angry.

When the meeting was over, I felt "fleshly good" because I was able to address some concerns; however, and the truth is, the meeting was unproductive and did not please our Father. Sadly, the bitter divide between us swelled and the wall between our churches grew taller and thicker.

Over the next several years the conflict between us and our churches brewed and simmered. The enemy loved that we didn't care for each other.

I will come back to Pastor Don in a minute. But first let me tell you about our church building.

Our church building is quite large. At one time it was the largest "free-standing" building in our county at 144,000 square feet. A pastor's worst nightmare is a leaking roof; well, our roof started to leak. Not in one simple, fixable place but dozens of leaks throughout the building. We did the best to patch the holes; but when we would fix one leak, three new ones would take its place. It was a complete nightmare. Every time it rained the water dripped on the people below.

During one of our weekly services, our worship team was singing a song that included the lyric "Let it rain, let it rain, let it rain." I kid you not. While we were singing that song…I was thinking to myself, *No, no, no, not that song,* because it was actually starting to rain outside. You can only guess what happened. That night a new guest was attending and happened to be sitting in the "perfect spot." When I heard the pitter patter of rain hitting the roof, I thought, *Oh no, please God don't let the roof leak now. We have guests in the building. Close the heavens like you did with Elijah. Heal our broken roof, clog the holes. Lap up the water on the roof with fire as you did in the Old Testament…send us a drought, please God!* Well, He didn't answer my prayer. It was awful. I just closed my eyes and hoped for the best.

God must have a sense of humor.

Just as we were singing those beautiful lyrics, our wonderful precious guest starting feeling the subtle splashes of rain. Being new, she had no idea we had leaks. Throughout the song, every few seconds a gentle splash of water would land on her. She thought she was touched with a physical encounter from the Lord, because immediately after the service she quickly ran up to me and said, "Pastor, you're not going to believe this, but while we were singing that song about let it rain, I actually felt it rain on me. I felt literal water. Isn't God so good? He is here! Praise Him!"

You can only imagine what I was thinking. The complexity of that moment was priceless.

As she talked and was overwhelmed by her heavenly encounter, my mind was navigating through a thousand thoughts. I simply smiled and nodded my head in agreement as if I believed her. I was speechless as well as devastated. I thought to myself, *What do I do? Do I tell her what she actually felt wasn't the Spirit of God, but real rain? Do I pray for her? Do I tell her it wasn't the Lord?* The more she talked, the more I smiled and the more I was dying on the inside. She was so adamant about her encounter. Again, what do I say?

Don't judge me too harshly. She was so excited and touched by the experience I didn't have the heart to tell her it was actual rainwater falling upon her because of our leaky roof. I just couldn't dampen her encounter. I have no doubt the Lord is going to ask me about this when I get to Heaven.

I was so embarrassed as I walked away crying out for God to help us and to bless His sweet daughter! I never saw her again.

You can imagine that I watched the weather more closely. I became a weather expert diagnosing the weather patterns, cold fronts, humidity, and moisture levels from the gulf coast. I would even create my own weather forecasts. If the meteorologist forecasted rain for Sundays, I immediately began to speak to the weather. I constantly prayed that God would not let it rain on Sundays, especially during Sunday night revival services.

Our leadership team knew we had to do something about the leaks, so we got estimates to replace the entire roof; the lowest bid we received was $288,000. We didn't have the money. Our church was already servicing a debt and we couldn't add any more to our monthly payment.

Our elders decided something had to be done and chose to repair half the roof—the cost, $144,000. The owner of the roofing company graciously allowed us to pay for the roof in six monthly installments rather than all at once.

I knew we didn't have enough money to replace the roof—we barely had enough income to manage our debt and pay our bills. I didn't know how we were going to come up with an additional $25,000 a month. I was concerned but not stressed. We were in revival and revival changes everything. My perspective was altered and things that used to bother me no longer did. In my heart, this was an opportunity for God to be God.

During a time of prayer and isolation in the sanctuary, I felt compelled by the Holy Spirit that we needed to plant a financial seed somewhere. I had been taught that if what you have can't meet your need, then it is time to plant a seed. It was no secret, all of our leaders knew we needed a financial miracle in order to replace the roof.

I had heard that Pastor Don's church, The Church at War Hill, was in a building program; to be honest, I was more envious than I would like to admit. So it surprised me when the Lord spoke to my heart and said, "I want you to sow seed into The Church of War Hill's new building program." No way was I expecting to hear God say give money to our archrival; perhaps a missionary in

China, a homeless ministry, or better yet a prison ministry—but not the "rattlesnake" preacher three and half miles down the road.

Again, revival changes everything, and the Lord was softening my heart on all fronts. Offenses and hurts were falling away from me; and surprisingly, I wasn't resistant to His request, just surprised. I said, "Okay, Lord." I immediately met with our elders and told them the Lord wanted us to sow a financial blessing into their church. They all agreed and felt it was God. The only thing left to decide was the amount.

I was thinking as well as all of the elders, except one, that a couple thousand dollars was more than enough. Brian Norris, who had been at the church for a long time, said, "The Lord is dropping into my spirit $50,000." When he said the amount, my spirit latched onto it and I knew it was God. However, we wanted to pray and make sure it was God and not us. The next week we met again; and after discussing the full spectrum of possibilities both positive and negative, we voted to move forward with the $50,000 gift to Pastor Don's church.

Miraculously, I no longer felt animosity and hostility toward Pastor Don Allen. I was filled with love and a deep desire to see him and his church succeed.

Before we delivered the $50,000 check to The Church at War Hill, each elder carried the check for a twenty-four hour period, praying over the seed and asking God to bless The Church at War Hill.

The day came for us to plant the seed. Pastor Marty, our executive pastor, and a small team traveled to Pastor Don's church and asked for a few minutes to address the congregation. Think about the unusualness of our request—it's not every day a group from a competing church walks in and wants to take the microphone to address their church on a Sunday morning. Thankfully, they reluctantly agreed to allow our team to address the congregation.

Pastor Marty took the mic and the room became eerily quiet; no one but our team knew what was about to happen. After a few opening remarks, he declared that Christ Fellowship Church wanted to sow a seed into their church and help them build their new building. They were shocked. When he presented the check and notified them of the amount, the congregation immediately applauded, shouted, wept and wailed. It was a divine Kingdom moment for them and us. Instantly, the animosity, competition, and disagreements between our churches vanished.

The Kingdom had come and our churches were united. The glory of God fell in their building and ours as well.

When revival comes to a church, it ultimately brings unity between pastors and their churches.

The seed sown continues to bring in a financial harvest. The harvest was so great the entire roof, $288,000, was paid for without ever borrowing any money. God met every need and then some more. To God be the glory!

8

BIRTHING TWO BABIES

*"When the Spirit is doing something new and
fresh, the greatest gift is not knowing how
to lead, but knowing how to follow."*
—RICK JOYNER

I'm not one to have dreams; however, in the early morning I
was awakened due to a disturbing dream. God often encourages His children via dreams and can even warn them of things to
come. I believe this is what happened to me.

The Dream

I found myself in the back seat of a car; it was dark and I had just given birth to a baby. I looked down and I was sitting on the baby, which was barely alive and even could have been dead. I knew the child's life was gone or in great peril. I was startled, and when I lifted myself off the baby it caught its breath and came back to life. Then I discovered I had given birth to another baby who was struggling as well; and again when I realized I was sitting on it, I lifted myself off and it too began to breathe again.

It is significant to know this dream took place two days after what I am about to share.

I must admit the following experience is really embarrassing. Usually, I would hesitate sharing this type of information, but I believe it will help many people. Here it goes.

I hate to admit to you that I almost killed the revival.

There is a sign on a highway that read: "It takes 3,500 bolts to put a car together, but only one nut to wreck it." Well, I was that one nut. You see, the North Georgia Revival almost came to a screeching halt not because of the devil, but me.

Here's how. Hosting a long-term move of God comes with a tremendous amount of pressure. I became consumed with creating the right environment in order to host the Lord well. People from all around the world who paid a tremendous price, walk through the doors and come to the altars expecting to receive their miracle or breakthrough. Plus, there was the training of new workers, building maintenance, managing staff, security issues, childcare, not to mention the financial pressures.

Karen and I have contended for a move of God like the North Georgia Revival for our entire Christian life. When the revival started, everyone knew we were having an authentic encounter with Heaven, and I had a naive expectation that our entire church would be on board with what God was doing.

Four months into the revival and I was frustrated on two significant fronts.

One, not everyone from church was attending the Sunday evening services where God was truly manifesting His power and glory. This baffled me to the point that I would become angry. It led to some interesting conversations between Karen and I. For the life of me I couldn't imagine staying home, going shopping, or being on the lake and missing an opportunity to encounter God and His glory. Again, these were not usual "revival" services; no, we were seeing unprecedented miracles every Sunday night— God was showing up.

Two, financially the church was struggling to keep up with the unexpected expenditures that came with revival. The demands were greater than our income; we were going into the hole nearly every week.

Things Get Bad

I had asked Karen to preach one Sunday morning, but before she preached I was to give a few announcements and take up the morning offering. All was well, but something shifted while I was giving the announcements—and it wasn't good. Evidently at that exact moment I had reached the boiling point and I took the opportunity to release some pent-up frustration. I hadn't planned on doing this, but it just started coming out.

I was frank and to the point. I told the congregation I was disappointed in many of them staying home and acting as if the revival was no big deal while the rest of the church was working extremely hard to host the Lord and the community. I called them out on it.

Second, I rebuked them for not financially supporting the revival. I revealed to them we were losing money and that I and the church could no longer do this. I emphatically said, "I will shut down the revival if you don't want it and if things don't improve." To say I moved from love to anger is an understatement. In the spirit, I think I grew a pointed tail, two horns, and had a pitchfork in my hand. I said what was on my mind and held nothing back.

Here's the crazy part. When I stepped down I felt good, I mean really good. All of the suppressed frustration spewed out of me and it felt wonderful.

After my seven-minute tirade, I had the privilege of introducing the guest speaker that morning, my beautiful wife. I handed her the microphone and she graciously smiled at me, but I knew it was fake. I wouldn't know how fake until later. And with her eyes she said to me, "What in the world have you just done?" In the moment her current thought was, *How can I salvage this service?* She knew I had blown it and the people were hurt. Karen was wonderful, she maintained her poise and preached a masterpiece.

As I sat down in the front row, I truly was oblivious about what I had done. In fact, as mentioned earlier, I was feeling pretty good about the beatdown I just delivered. However, the more I sat there, the more I began to realize God was not pleased with my actions.

When the church service ended, I left immediately. That afternoon I began preparing to receive evangelist Pat Schatzline who was scheduled to preach that evening for the revival. At that time we were baptizing an average of 30-40 people each Sunday evening service.

When Pat arrived on our campus and entered the sanctuary, he could tell something was different about the atmosphere. He forged ahead and preached a great message and even gave a stirring altar call and encouraged people to come encounter Jesus in the baptismal waters. The people just stood there that night we baptized only three people. This was not good.

Up to this point Pat had ministered at the revival multiple times and was familiar with the typical level of glory in the room. He was puzzled. He couldn't put his finger on what had caused the shift in the room. He looked at me and I acted like I didn't know either, but I did.

It didn't take long for Pat to find out because Karen told him. On the way to taking Pat to his hotel, I had to stop and get gas. When I exited the car to pump the gas, Karen and Pat remained in the car and she ratted me out—she told him all that I had done that morning. She not only threw me under the bus, she was driving the bus and ran over me multiple times. She gave no mercy, none.

When I got back in the car, Pat asked me what happened in the morning service. Wow, that was quick. I knew I was busted. I confessed and told him what I said to the people. Pat looked at me while I was driving and said, "Bro, you can't do that." And for about forty-five minutes he mentored me on how to pastor a move of God. I agreed with him that I was wrong and committed to making it right with the people. I told Pat and Karen that I would apologize to the church.

The Lord revealed to me that, like Moses, I had *struck* the rock rather than *speak* to the rock.

The following Sunday I couldn't apologize to the church due to the direction of the service; it just wouldn't fit. I was kinda relieved, and I also was hoping the Lord would give me a pass on this one. He didn't. So, you guessed it, the atmosphere at our Sunday night revival service was still not right. The level of glory was down and that evening we only baptized four people. I was greatly troubled in my heart.

Deep down I knew I had to apologize to the people for my fleshly rant on that dreadful Sunday morning. I conveniently made plans to apologize on the following Wednesday evening church service. Before I started my message, I gave a heartfelt confession and I humbly asked their forgiveness for striking the rock on Sunday morning.

After the service I was feeling pretty good about what I had done. People were admiring my vulnerability and appreciative that I would even admit that I had done wrong.

While they were supporting my actions, I felt an uneasiness in my spirit. And when the crowd left, I asked the Lord, "Why do I still feel convicted and uneasy in my heart?" He said, "Todd, you didn't say those things on a Wednesday night."

I knew exactly what He wanted me to do. It was on a Sunday morning when I verbally lashed out at my congregation and I needed to confess on the same platform and service time— Sunday morning. Oh my, He was really working on me.

The following Sunday came and I was nervous but knew what I needed to do. When I stood to preach I shared with my people what the Lord spoke to me on Wednesday night and immediately confessed my shortcoming to the Sunday morning crowd. With tears I asked my church family to forgive me. They did.

I had no idea what the evening revival service would be like. I was nervous that the downward trend would continue, but it didn't. As soon I walked into the sanctuary that evening I could tell something was different...the atmosphere was electric and explosive. God's presence was obvious and His glory unmistakable; once again we baptized more than forty people. The revival was back on track!

Back to the dream. There is where God revealed to me that through my actions I was sitting on the revival and was killing it. I truly believe if I had not repented, the revival would have come to a stop. God would have pulled back His glory.

I learned a valuable lesson: I must be sensitive to His voice and be quick to repent both to Him and others.

Part Two

HEAVEN'S TREASURES

9

WHAT IS THE GLORY OF GOD?

"If you are in a church that is allowing you to be free to do anything you like, RUN FOR YOUR LIFE! If you are not in a church that is preaching the whole gospel, all the words in red, RUN FOR YOUR LIFE!"
—Evangelist Steve Hill

What is the glory of God?

The glory of God is an expansive subject and as you shall see, has a broad variety of definitions. However, we will dissect the word *glory* in order to understand its application to our lives.

The word *glory* appears in the Old Testament more than 140 times. Traditionally and in many texts of the Bible, glory is understood to mean greatness, praise for the Lord, magnificence, brilliance, grandeur, beauty, brightness, fame, splendor, and even honor.

Here are some examples:

- First Chronicles 16:28-29: *"Give to the Lord, O families of the peoples, give to the Lord glory and strength. Give to the Lord the glory due His name...."*
- Jeremiah 13:16: *"Give glory to the Lord your God...."*
- Psalm 62:7: *"In God is my salvation and my glory...."*
- Joshua 7:19: *"...give glory to the Lord...."*
- Nehemiah 9:5: *"...blessed be Your glorious name...."*

The phrase *"glory of God"* should not be limited to just these biblical expressions and definitions; in fact, it has a much broader usage than what most people know. In addition, it is important to note that the glory of God is not the Holy Spirit, nor is it a person.

I would like you to take a moment and meditate on the following Scriptures that mention a different element of the glory of God:

> *Then Moses went up into the mountain, and a cloud covered the mountain. Now the **glory of the Lord** rested on Mount Sinai, and the cloud covered it six days. And on the seventh day He called to Moses out of the midst of the cloud (Exodus 24:15-16).*

*And you said: "Surely the Lord our **God has shown us His glory** and His greatness, and we have heard His voice from the midst of the fire..."* (Deuteronomy 5:24).

*Then the cloud covered the tabernacle of meeting, and the **glory of the Lord filled the tabernacle**. And Moses was not able to enter the tabernacle of meeting, because the cloud rested above it, and the **glory of the Lord filled the tabernacle*** (Exodus 40:34-35).

*And it came to pass, when the priests came out of the holy place, that the cloud filled the house of the Lord, so that the priests could not continue ministering because of the cloud; **for the glory of the Lord filled the house of the Lord*** (1 Kings 8:10-11).

*So I have looked for You in the sanctuary, **to see Your power and Your glory*** (Psalm 63:2).

It is worth mentioning that the Hebrew Bible in multiple places reveals that the glory of God is the *kovod* of God. *Kovod* means weight, not just a little amount of weight but a heavy weight. It has substance, a thickness. Therefore, the glory is the weightiness of the Lord. Again, the glory is not a person but an essence, it is like the residue of God. I liken it to humidity; it can be felt, experienced, and at times seen.

*Now it came to pass, as Aaron spoke to the whole congregation of the children of Israel, that they looked toward the wilderness, and behold, **the glory of the Lord appeared** in the cloud* (Exodus 16:10).

Tommy Tenney equates the glory of God to "His visible weighty presence."

John Kilpatrick says, "It can be felt."

Duncan Campbell defines glory "as a community saturated with God."

Rick Warren declares, "It is the essence of His nature, the weight of His importance; the radiance of His splendor...the atmosphere of His presence."

When discussing the glory, we are revealing the full nature, essence, and character of God; and when that glory is present, the atmosphere and interactions with God are completely different. No one is ever the same after coming up under the weightiness of God.

Moses approached the Lord and requested that God be with him as he led the people of Israel into the Promised Land. Then Moses made a bodacious and unthinkable request to God, *"Please show me Your glory."* What? Did Moses just go there? Has Moses lost his mind? Think about it, Moses was petitioning God to show him His unfiltered, unbridled, unapproachable essence. God knew the magnitude and terrible consequences of Moses' desire and spoke:

> *"I will make all My goodness pass before you...." But He said, "You cannot see My face; for no man shall see Me, and live." And the Lord said, "Here is a place by Me, and you shall stand on the rock. So it shall be, while **My glory** passes by, that I will put you in the cleft of the rock, and will cover you with My hand while I pass by.*

Then I will take away My hand, and you shall see My back; but My face shall not be seen" (Exodus 33:19-23).

God basically told Moses, "I will have to cover your face with My hand as I walk by and I will only allow you to see My back side; in other words, the aftereffects of My presence, the residue."

This is fascinating on many levels. I find it interesting that Moses was so hungry for the glory of God that he was willing to die to encounter it.

Are we?

WE MUST!

10

WHAT HAPPENS WHEN GOD'S GLORY COMES?

In February, three weeks after having the vision of fire on the water, God's glory entered our building. It was a Sunday night service. We decided to come back together in the evening because there was an unusual level of the presence of God in our morning service. God met us; His presence was even stronger in the evening than in the morning.

The worship was so intimate and tender; and as I always do after the praise and worship set, I made my way to the platform to transition the service and take up an offering and introduce our guest speaker. However, because of His presence being so strong,

I knelt on the platform to soak in His beauty and to simply love on Him some more. His presence was overwhelming.

After a few minutes I chose to lay on my back before the Lord, I wanted this moment to last forever. The longer I was there, the more He increased His glory. Multiple times I tried to get up off the platform to address my people, but I couldn't, I was unable to move my torso. I had use of my hands and legs, but that was it. For thirty minutes I was unable to get up. The weight of God's glory was sitting on me; it felt like a thousand pounds was on my chest.

There was immense joy and peace, as well as a holy fear. Tears streamed down my face as I was succumbed by His glory. A few of the leaders became concerned and came to check on me, because this was so unlike my nature. They kept asking me what do we need to do about the service? I responded, "Obey the Holy Spirit, let Him move." They did. God came and changed all of us.

What Happened Next?

People often say they want revival and desire an encounter with the glory of God. I respect this and rejoice with them. However, people need to understand that God's intention for us is much more than giving us a physical or emotional experience. The initial exposure to His glory was otherworldly, even to this day it is difficult to articulate the wonder of it. However, there is more to it than being wowed by His goodness and glory.

I want to answer the question, "What happens to the people and the church when God's glory comes?" The result is interesting. The following is the process my church and I went through.

1. The Glory of God Stimulates Your Entire Person

When the glory of God rested upon our church, we were all in wonder of God's magnificent presence. At no time in my life had I felt and witnessed God's presence like I did. Often, I would walk into the sanctuary and kneel immediately; at times I would laugh and then cry. It was glorious. At times, my body felt like it was in Heaven, and at other times it was difficult to breathe due to the weightiness of His presence.

Our church services were like an oasis in the desert. I watched as thirsty, broken and dry people would come and drink deeply from the fountain of living water. They would kneel at the altar and encounter God—and within minutes they would stand up new people. The joy and peace was unexplainable.

Typically, in the beginning of revival there is a sweet brokenness on the people as God's tender presence pushes into those who are present. Graciously, God begins to show us the obvious areas of our lives that we and others know need to be changed. For the most part, people willingly submit to the conviction of the Holy Spirit and repent. Most of the people in the church in this stage are on board because their friends, distant prodigals, and those who are marginal in their relationship with Jesus encounter Him at the altar. Everyone is rejoicing and happy and can't wait to attend the next service.

2. The Glory of God Sanctifies Believers

Warning: This stage is painful! It is not as exciting as the previous stage, but more necessary. His presence is still felt when you walk in, but the glory and Spirit of God have a different agenda: the sanctification of the believers who attend the church. God's goal in this stage is to prepare His children for lasting change that will enable them to host His glory long term. Remember, God's purpose is not for visitation, but habitation. This stage is an absolute must if habitation is to occur. Ironically, it is here, stage two, that the church decides to what degree they want God to move. Do they want visitation or habitation? Sadly, for various reasons most moves of God don't make it past this stage.

Why?

God goes to work on our flesh. He goes deep, beyond the obvious and begins to point out the hidden areas of our lives that no one else knows or even thinks is a problem. In stage one God works on the obvious issues in our lives; not here, no, in stage two He goes beyond the surface. At this point, just as a master surgeon who cuts away flesh to find infection, God uncovers the layers of our heart and exposes our deeply rooted infections that have been hidden from the public eye.

It is here many people exit revival, the revival they supported in the beginning. God puts pressure on their flesh and it becomes hard for them to adjust to the demands He is asking from them. So, instead of remaining under the weight of His glory, they remove themselves. I witnessed this firsthand at our revival; it broke my heart as I watched people walk away from the work of sanctification going on in their lives, and subsequently the glory of God.

In revival this process of sanctification is unavoidable; it is part of God's plan. Those who submit to God's plan and die to themselves will make it through the process with a greater dimension of purity and power. They become adequate hosts and conduits for His glory.

3. The Glory of God Will Shock You

When we came out of the arduous sanctification stage, God started revealing a dimension of His power we had never witnessed before—it shocked us! His power was on display.

We starting seeing legitimate verifiable miracles take place right in front of us. People we knew were receiving physical healings that baffled us all and even those in the medical profession. For example, one night I had a very short dream. I saw one of the members of my church holding his jaw as if he was having a dental problem. I woke up and the Lord said to me, "I want you to pray for people this Sunday who have dental issues." I thought that was unusual. I had never prayed for people's dental issues before, but I obeyed. Sunday came and I shared with the people my dream, then I asked, "If you have a dental issue, come forward to receive prayer." I was amazed as nearly one hundred people came to the altar.

A precious lady who needed denture implants responded to the call for prayer. Previously her dentist told her she didn't have enough bone in her jaw to successfully do the procedure. That day she received prayer and a few weeks later went back to the dentist for another evaluation. After the x-rays, the dentist sat down with her and he asked, "Do you believe in miracles?" She said, "Yes I do, we are in revival at my church." He replied, "You have thirty percent new bone growth!" This was a miracle!

Miracles like this and others were taking place almost every week. For example, cancers were healed, incurable diseases vanished, deaf ears opened, mental disorders were eradicated, self-inflicted scars disappeared—these are just a few of the unprecedented miracles we saw. To say we were being shocked by all that we were witnessing is an epic understatement. It was as if the book of Acts was coming alive in our church.

I am convinced the level of miracles we were seeing would not have manifested if we hadn't submitted to the process of being sanctified.

> And Joshua said to the people, "Sanctify yourselves, for tomorrow the Lord will do wonders among you" (Joshua 3:5).

4. The Glory of God Will Bring Separation

Hosting the presence of God takes a tremendous amount of effort and can be taxing on you physically as well as the church body as a whole. It requires long hours as people from all around the world will want to come and encounter His presence. Furthermore, God will do things in your midst that others, those on the outside of the revival, will not understand. Therefore, because they don't understand, they will call into question the authenticity of the move and doubt the biblical validity of such manifestations. Naturally, the outcome will be separation. People will begin to isolate themselves from you. They still love you but cannot walk with you on this journey.

Don't worry, this is what happens in every significant long-term revival. After all, it even happened to Jesus. For instance, whenever He would require a greater sacrifice and commitment from people and His disciples, many responded negatively. They stopped following Him; they separated themselves from Him. The Bible records, *"From that time many of His disciples went back and walked with Him no more"* (John 6:66). It is worthy to note that earlier in the day, the Bible says that *"a great multitude followed Him, because they saw His signs which He performed on those who were diseased"* (John 6:2). Many of His followers loved the fact that He was doing good and healing the sick; however, the moment He asked for more, they distanced themselves from Him and His work. No matter how glorious God's work is, not everyone is willing to pay the price to walk with Him.

Please hear my heart—I want you to be prepared because this will happen to you. The greater the glory on your life, expect the greater the separation from others—others who truly love you, but don't quite understand your new expression of commitment to and love for Jesus. You have to be willing to leave people behind as you progress further. Don't allow the confusion of others or their carnality or even genuine concern for you keep you from encountering and living in His glory. I once heard Bill Johnson say, "The closer to God you get, the less you can take with you."

God is raising up an army of believers who are willing to do whatever He asks and pay whatever price necessary to encounter and walk in His glory. You can be comforted in knowing as you faithfully walk through each stage, the level of glory intensifies. Let us go from glory to glory!

> *But we all, with unveiled face, beholding as in a mirror the glory of the Lord, are being transformed into the same image **from glory to glory**, just as by the Spirit of the Lord* (2 Corinthians 3:18).

11

THE GLORY CAN COME AND GO

*"When may a revival be expected? When the wickedness
of the wicked grieves and distresses the Christian."*
—BILLY SUNDAY

In First Samuel 4, the people of God were attacked and
soundly defeated by the Philistines. When the pregnant daughter-in-law of Eli the high priest received word that her husband
was slain while in battle and that the Ark of God was also captured by the enemy, she *"...bowed herself and gave birth, for her
labor pains came upon her"* (1 Samuel 4:19).

Evidently, she was so traumatized by the news she immediately went into labor and gave birth to a son. Scriptures reveal she died shortly thereafter; but before she passed, she named her son Ichabod, meaning the *"glory* [of God] *has departed from Israel"* (1 Samuel 4:22).

The word *ichabod* means "inglorious" or "the glory is no more." Wow, what a word picture. With the naming of her son she recognized and declared that the glory, the substance of God, was gone from Israel.

It has never been God's will to withdraw His glory from His people and Church, but sometimes we give Him no other option. Many scholars believe Adam and Eve were clothed in glory in the Garden of Eden. His glory was their covering, but when they chose to rebel against God, His glory lifted and immediately they recognized they were naked.

I wonder how many churches used to have the glory of God in their midst, but over time have lost it? I venture to say, some have lost the glory and don't even know it. They keep operating, doing church as usual and have no clue that His glory is no more.

I believe the very issues that caused the departure of the glory of God in Eli's day are the same issues that will cause God to "pull back" His glory from the local church. For example, dishonor, indifference, a disregard for holiness, carnality among the leadership, rebellion, compromise, and willful disobedience.

Again, we are not talking about His *presence* departing, but His *glory,* for God is always with us, He is forever present. But, His glory can lift and depart from an individual or church, meaning His weightiness and heavy substance can pull away.

I know personally, through years of ministerial activity, that you can have the Spirit of God present in your life and church—but

not encounter a deep level of the glory of God. You can even oper-
ate in the anointing of the Spirit and not experience the glory of
God. I know this may seem impossible, but it is definitely possible.

The glory of God is not just a cloud, even though it can manifest that way. I have been in services at the North Georgia Revival
and didn't see any physical manifestation at all other than feel the
heaviness, the weight of God pressing onto us. It was undeniable.
There have been multiple times when I have been unable to move
due to the heavenly weight on my body.

We have discovered the glory of God doesn't come by a commitment to do better or fulfilling resolutions. God sends His glory
to a church for multiple reasons; however in my opinion, when
people gather together for prayer and cry out for all of Him, God
responds. In measure, God is attracted to our activities of preaching, teaching, and singing—but nothing moves God like prayer.

God's Glory on a City

In the midst of the Welsh Revival, which began in 1904, it was
reported that men would avoid going to their homes and make
their way to the local bars to drink because they knew the presence
of God was in their homes due to their praying wives. However,
the Lord graciously met them in the bars. It was reported by many
that as the men would lift their glass to their lips, an unseen hand
would stop them from drinking, and they knew it was God's hand
and would quickly run to their homes and repent before the Lord
and were saved.

As the revival fire spread and intensified, people around the
world came to see and experience the work of God. Once, some

out-of-town visitors were seeking directions to one of the meetings in Wales. The guests were told to take the train. The visitors asked, "How will we know when we are there?" The reply, "You will feel it." And they did! After leaving the train, the same guests asked a stranger for directions to the building hosting the revival meeting. They were given vague directions. Again they asked, "But how we will know where to turn?" The answer, "You'll feel it!" And they did!

When the glory is present, everyone knows it, even the unsaved. It's undeniable.

Her Scary List!

She came out of nowhere. She quietly sat down next to me at the altar. She said nothing. I just finished preaching and was talking to a young man about the Lord. I knew she was there to talk so I turned and looked at her.

Her face spoke volumes; her skin was typical for a twenty-seven-year old, childlike in appearance—but the eyes. The eyes told a different story. Her eyes vividly revealed the bewildered inner chambers of her soul—the pain, heartache, mental torture, disappointment, and despair. Jesus said, *"Your eyes are the windows into your body"* (Matthew 6:22 The Message).

At first she said nothing but handed me a folded church tithing envelope that obviously was held onto tightly and compressed repeatedly in her hands. It wasn't an offering, no, it was the only piece of paper she found. During the service she chronicled her life, and the carefully chosen words on the back side of the envelope were her current reality.

Her list:

- PTSD
- Porn addiction
- Sexual sin
- Prostitution
- Heart problems
- Raped
- OCD (germs)
- Shame
- Fear
- Unworthy
- Bisexual
- Adultery
- Facing divorce
- Depression
- All forgotten sins
- All sickness-illness
- Muscle spasms
- Body weakness
- Infertility

As I clung to the envelope in my hands, I kept staring at the list and it broke my heart. Never had I seen within one person this level of pain and debilitating issues. Then it went to the next level and I was unprepared for what she said.

PTSD was at the top of the list; it caught my eye. I questioned her, "Why PTSD, what happened?"

"It was the perfect storm," she said. "When I was seventeen, I came out of my bedroom and turned the corner and entered the living room. My dad was sitting in his chair. He had a gun, and as soon as I looked at him, he pulled the trigger and killed himself."

Now all the other things on the list made perfect sense. I got it. Not justifying it, but I understood. My heart was filled with compassion. Her whole life had been about survival and coping with horrors no human should experience or see, especially a child.

As she shared her story she wept tears poisoned with unimaginable heartache. Then with anguish she added, "Every night I have nightmares. I can't get rid of them. In my mind, I see the suicide over and over."

I could hear the desperation in her voice and see the misery in her eyes. Those eyes looked at me as if to say, "Can you help me? Can you do anything for me? I don't want to be like this anymore." I knew by experience that in the natural it would take fifty years of counseling to free her from all of her struggles.

A sense of profound hopelessness came over me as I felt completely exposed and unqualified. It was a moment of truth for me. I humbly confessed I couldn't do anything for her. She looked puzzled at my honesty. I knew I was no match for the giants in her life both physically and spiritually. However, I quickly responded and emphatically pointed her to the baptismal pool…the vision I had of fire on the water was for moments like these. With all the faith I had I assured her as soon as her foot touched the water, Jesus would meet her there. I didn't doubt for one second that Jesus would minister to her. I had witnessed it thousands of times and was fully convinced He would do it again.

Before she left the altar to get in line to be baptized, we prayed. His presence came upon her as she tenderly wept and repented to the Lord. She was baptized later that evening and encountered His power—He met her!

I wanted to know what drew her to the service. She said, "My mom brought me. She heard what Jesus was doing and wanted to come see."

"How is your mom…is she following Jesus?" I asked.

"No, she's an addict," she replied.

"What is she addicted to?" I asked.

"Everything!"

Isn't it interesting that addicts are hearing about the supernatural deliverances and healings taking place in the baptismal waters and are inviting each other to church? Sinners are inviting sinners to encounter His glory. These are great times.

May the Church be ready!

12

BRONZE VERSUS GOLD

*"Modern Christianity has been watered down until the
solution is so weak that if it were poison it would not hurt
anyone, and if it were medicine it would not cure anyone."*
—A.W. Tozer

Gold is a prized commodity. People worldwide understand the value it holds.

Michael Phelps, a United States swimmer from 2004-2016,
won more gold medals than anyone in the history of the Olympic
games, twenty-three to be exact.

Did you know the gold medal isn't actually solid gold? It is made up of 92 percent silver and has six grams of gold that plates the metal. The last Olympic gold medal made from solid gold was awarded in 1912 in Stockholm. After that year, the gold medals have been gilded silver rather than solid gold.[1] It looks like gold, shines like gold, and is portrayed as gold, but it is actually just silver covered in gold.

One of the largest cash robberies in the United States occurred in 1997 when five friends collaborated and robbed the Dunbar Armored Car facility in Los Angeles, California. Their plan was executed flawlessly and were successful in stealing $18.9 million. The leader of the gang was Allen Pace, who worked for Dunbar as a regional safety inspector. He knew all the details on how to avoid the security cameras and who and when the guards would be moving throughout the facility. Pace carefully recruited four of his childhood friends to help him with the heist. After success-fully robbing his company, they hid the money until things settled down. However, after a long investigation, all five were arrested—but most of the money that was stolen has not been recovered.

Stealing $18.9 million is a significant amount of money, yet it is not much compared to the theft that took place in First Kings 14. King Solomon, David's son, was the richest man in all of his-tory and responsible for building the royal palace and the temple in Jerusalem. Solomon accepted the mandate and in doing so spared no expense. The royal palace and temple were exquisite to say the least, and an enormous amount of gold and jewels were the bedrock of these two structures.

Together they were the most luxurious man-made buildings in the known world, and they were filled with magnificent treasures that reflected the blessing and glory of Solomon's kingdom. The temple alone took 186,000 laborers seven and one-half years to construct. It is estimated that to build that temple today would cost more than $50 billion.

As a reference to the temple's majesty, while Solomon was still king, the Queen of Sheba visited him and said,

> *It was a true report which I heard in my own land about your words and your wisdom. However I did not believe the words until I came and saw with my own eyes; and indeed the half was not told me. Your wisdom and prosperity exceed the fame of which I heard* (1 Kings 10:6-7).

Life was amazing under Solomon's reign; however, after his death, David's grandson Rehoboam inherited the kingdom. Immediately Rehoboam committed sin and rebelled against God. Up to this point Israel had basically been impenetrable, but Rehoboam's rebellion opened the door for Israel to be attacked by their enemies, specifically Egypt.

The king of Egypt recognized Israel's vulnerability and quickly moved, overwhelming Israel's army with superior strength and force. According to Second Chronicles 12, King Shishak's army in part consisted of 60,000 horsemen, 1,200 chariots, and an innumerable number of foot soldiers. The Egyptians without restraint pillaged Israel and took all the prized valuables. Shishak wasn't satisfied with the jewels of the common man, he had his eye on something of immense value—the gold inside the royal palace and Solomon's temple. More specifically, the 300 shields of gold that Solomon had made for the soldiers guarding the palace and temple.

Shishak wanted to rob the gold shields from King Rehoboam not only because of their monetary value but also what they represented to the people of Israel—the glory, favor, and presence of God. He wanted to take it all away from the people of God. We can only imagine the splendor of such shields as guards stood at attention protecting the house of the king and the house of God. It was a spectacular and reflective demonstration of the greatness and beauty of the God of Israel. Each shield was covered with three pounds of gold valued at $160,000 apiece. The shields collectively were worth approximately $50 million.[2]

Shishak indeed pillaged the people and the temple: *"And he took away the treasures of the house of the Lord and the treasures of the king's house; he took away everything. He also took away all the gold shields which Solomon had made"* (1 Kings 14:26). He took the 300 shields of gold that were significant to the king and the house of the Lord. He took the symbols that represented the glory and majesty of God.

The significance of this story is what King Rehoboam did after the gold was taken from the palace and the temple. Instead of replacing the shields with gold, he instructed his laborers to make shields and cover them with bronze. That's right, he settled for bronze because it was cheaper and easier and it also gave the appearance of real gold.

It was to look like gold but it wasn't. The bronze would shine like gold but it wasn't. To the eye no one could tell it was bronze, why? They kept it polished and looking nice, but in reality the glory and splendor of the temple was gone.

In general, I think this is what has happened to the Church— the gold (glory) is virtually gone, somewhere along the way we lost it. Whether we misplaced it or it was stolen is immaterial, the fact is, the glory is not present in the vast majority of our churches, and to compensate for it we have done exactly what King Rehoboam did, we made shields of bronze. Our worship services under the flashing lights make our presentation look like gold; the words we use say we have gold, but it's mostly bronze. By and large our ministries shimmer and shine, and we portray ourselves as if we have gold, but if we are honest, it's mostly bronze, a lesser version and not the same.

Let me expound further. Again, I am not criticizing and being judgmental, I'm simply stating an opinion that is regretfully more accurate than not. The Church today is surrounded by bronze shields. Never has there been more talent on our platforms than now. Most of the people are attractive and look like they have their lives together. The pastors and communicators are by far the best in Christian history. Our programs and processes are exquisite and executed to perfection. People come into our services broken and desperate for an encounter with the glory of God. But instead of admitting our powerlessness that leaves people unchanged, we keep shining and waving our bronze shields, waving them for all the world to see.

Along the way we have settled for bronze rather than gold. We have convinced ourselves that there isn't much difference between the bronze shields and gold shields. At a distance they look the same; and because they look the same, we think they are the same. It is Second Timothy 3:5 on display, *"having a form of godliness but denying its power...."*

Over the past few decades, we have worked hard to present a great performance on Sundays to attract the community, and in doing so we have perfected our talent and approach. This is not wrong in and of itself; however, while doing so we haven't made the necessary sacrifices to attract *God* to our services. We have so been busy with the glitz, lights, haze, and perfection of ministry that we have lost our gold shield, His glory.

Sermons today give us principles, steps, and formulas to a happier life, but not a golden encounter with His glory, rather it's a bronze shield. We participate in worship that has more to do with talent and performance than it does His presence, bronze again. Our services on the weekend many times are like a show, a production that artfully displays our version and expression of Christianity. It lacks power and is an imitation of the real gospel of the Kingdom. It is impressive indeed, but has little to no power to confront the deep needs of the people much less thwart the enemy's advancement around the world.

God's people have to become desperate to reclaim what has been absent from our lives and churches. The good news—we know what the problem is and if we want it enough, we can change it. There is gold available and glory to be experienced. We have to forsake the fake and pursue the face of God.

We all know that in the natural mining for gold is not easy, you have to dig for it. In the spiritual, acquiring His glory gold requires a concerted effort and the willingness to keep digging until you strike gold. The effort will be worth it. We must not settle for bronze.

Dig, my friend, dig!

ENDNOTES

1. https://www.thoughtco.com/what-are-olympic-medals-made-of
    -608456; accessed May 17, 2020.
2. https://churchesofgod.info/article-what-did-happen-to-those
    -shields; accessed May 17, 2020.

13

THE ALTAR

"The important thing to remember is repentance is the prelude to revival. The church must first repent."

—J. Edwin Orr

hat touched the heart of God in the Old Testament still touches His heart today. He nor His expectations have changed.

My spirit hangs on every word of Second Chronicles 7. The most famous Scripture is verse 14, which unfolds the Father's heart concerning revival:

If my people, who are called by my name, will humble themselves and pray and seek my face and turn from their wicked ways, then I will hear from heaven, and I will forgive their sin and will heal their land.

However, many people skip over the first part of the chapter, which I believe reveals the pathway to walking in the manifest presence of God and His glory.

> *When **Solomon had finished praying,** fire came down from heaven and consumed the burnt offering and the sacrifices; and **the glory of the Lord** filled the temple. And the priests could not enter the house of the Lord, because **the glory of the Lord** had filled the Lord's house. When all the children of Israel saw how the fire came down, and **the glory of the Lord** on the temple, they bowed their faces to the ground on the pavement, and worshiped and praised the Lord, saying: "For He is good, for His mercy endures forever"* (2 Chronicles 7:1-3).

I am convinced that in order to experience the glory of God on your life, you first have to navigate and get acquainted with Him in an intimate way, like in verse 1 where four uncompromisable components are mentioned: 1) prayer; 2) an altar; 3) sacrifice; and 4) fire.

Tommy Tenney understood this and said, "Fire doesn't fall on empty altars. There has to be a sacrifice on the altar for the fire to fall. If you want the fire of God, you must become the fuel of God."

Oswald Chambers, who wrote the epic devotional, *My Utmost for His Highest,* said, "You must be willing to be placed on the altar and go through the fire; willing to experience what the altar represents—burning, purifications, and separation for only one purpose—the elimination of every desire and affection not grounded in or directed toward God."

It is a fact that when we come to the end of ourselves, then we have the opportunity to encounter a new realm of God and a new dimension of His glory. I witnessed this firsthand.

Samuel's Crooked Eye

I will never forget what happened to Samuel, a 10-year-old boy. He was not only born legally blind and had a crooked left eye, the doctors also told his parents to prepare themselves because their precious son would never be able to read as an adult. The reason? He had a severe form of dyslexia. When diagnosed, Samuel was in the third grade and reading on a kindergarten level.

One day as I shared my vivid vision of fire on the water and told the remarkable stories of the North Georgia Revival, I invited people to be baptized. More than 100 people responded—Samuel was one of them.

The presence of God was strong at Beth Hallel Synagogue in Birmingham, Alabama, and Samuel decided all by himself that he wanted to be baptized. His reason? He wanted his eyes to be healed. Rabbi David Schneier took Samuel by the hand as he slowly descended the steps into the water.

When he was immersed, Jesus met Samuel in the water. It was so sweet and powerful. When he came up out of the water he was visibly shaking. He trembled. I watched him and wanted to know what was going on in and around him. As he climbed the stairs, they placed a towel on his shoulders and gave him his glasses. He put his glasses on and immediately took them off and said, "These are not working anymore."

While in the water Jesus healed his eye and now Samuel has perfect vision. Jesus also straightened his crooked eye. The last time I talked to his parents, Samuel was reading on a third-grade level. God had also healed him of dyslexia!

Sadly, the altars in too many churches are used as steps to ascend onto the platform rather than a place to be burned by God's holy fire. This has to change; in biblical days the altar meant one thing—death.

Pay close attention to what happened in Second Chronicles 7:2: *"And the priests could not enter the house of the Lord, because the glory of the Lord had filled the Lord's house."* Because of Solomon's prayer, the proper use of the altar, and an acceptable sacrifice on the altar, the fire of God descended and the glory of God came. The result was remarkable. The priests could not enter the temple to perform their duties because the weight of God's glory rendered them helpless. Imagine that. The glory was so heavy that it neutralized all flesh and its activities.

When the general public saw how the radiant fire came from Heaven and the glory of God descended on the temple, they immediately fell on their faces and worshipped the Lord:

> *When all the children of Israel saw how the fire came down, and* ***the glory of the Lord*** *on the temple, they bowed their faces to the ground on the pavement, and worshiped and praised the Lord, saying: "For He is good, for His mercy endures forever"* (2 Chronicles 7:3).

I know this encounter may seem unordinary. You may even feel that this type of thing mentioned is limited to Bible days, but let me share with you a story that may change your mind.

Too Much God

Smith Wigglesworth was preaching in Wellington, New Zealand, when he summoned eleven leaders to attend a special prayer meeting. He allowed the members of the invited group to pray and then he rose to seek the face of the Lord. In a matter of a few minutes the glory of God filled the small room. The glory and the light became so bright and the heat so unbearable that one at a time all eleven men exited the room, they couldn't take it any longer. Wigglesworth was left alone in the room meeting with God.

Word quickly spread about the divine encounter. One local pastor who was unable to attend the first prayer service was determined to make it to the next one. He fearlessly committed not to leave the meeting regardless of how the strength of God's presence increased in the room.

At the next prayer meeting after the others had prayed, Wigglesworth began to worship and pray. Once again in short order, God filled the room and the weight of His glory settled upon the entire group. Just like before, all of the men abandoned the room except the one determined pastor. However, after Wigglesworth was caught up in the Spirit radiant with holy fire, the sincere minister could handle it no more and humbly withdrew from the room.

One pastor who crawled out of the room was asked what it was like in the room and why he left. Through tears and brokenness the pastor said, "There is too much God in that room."

Even though many Christians desire to experience the glory of God, I must add it does not come easily. In fact, the steps to His glory are a process, and at times the journey can be very difficult and even painful. Let me explain.

I don't mean to be redundant, but I must make it clear that God's glory is not cheap and will not come simply because we desire it—there is much more to it. To begin with, in order to experience God's glory we must pray, and prayer requires discipline. Second, an altar needs to be erected. These two are the easy elements. Here is when it gets difficult—a sacrifice is needed. Not only needed, but it must be placed on the altar. You and I must climb upon the altar and allow the fire of God to burn us until death.

Let me boldly interject—this level of encounter doesn't happen by casually walking up to the front of the church and having someone lay hands on you to impart the fire of God into and on you. That may be a good start, but it's not enough. You must place yourself on the altar and cry out, "God, burn everything out of me that doesn't please you. Consume me!"

Ultimately, death draws the attention of God, nothing else. Not our talent, our charming promises to do better next time— only absolute death.

Tommy Tenney, in his book *The God Chasers,* writes, "The more death God smells, the closer He can come."[1]

There is something about burning flesh that attracts God's attention.

Genesis 8:20-21: *"Then Noah built an altar to the Lord, and took of every clean animal and of every clean bird, and offered burnt offerings on the altar. And the Lord smelled a soothing aroma...."*

Leviticus 1:17: *"Then he shall split it at its wings, but shall not divide it completely; and the priest shall burn it on the altar, on the wood that is on the fire. It is a burnt sacrifice, an offering made by fire, a sweet aroma to the Lord."*

We have to come to end of ourselves, the utter end where there is nothing left. Crawl onto the altar and cry out to God, "Consume me!" This is the very reason we experience so little glory, because the price to have it is enormous.

ENDNOTE

1. Tommy Tenney, *The God Chasers*, (Shippensburg, PA: Destiny Image Publishers, 1998), 60.

14

PEARL OF GREAT PRICE

"It is an awful condition to be satisfied with one's spiritual attainments…God was and is looking for hungry, thirsty people."
—SMITH WIGGLESWORTH

In 2006, the world's largest and most expensive pearl in the world was discovered inside a clam by a Filipino fisherman off the coast of the Palawan Island, Philippines. The exotic pearl weighs an astounding 75 pounds and is 26 inches in length. In comparison, the average size pearl is 7 millimeter, or .3 inches. The fisherman put the pearl under his bed and there it remained for ten years—and remembered it only after a fire destroyed his small, humble home. At that time, in 2016, this gigantic pearl was valued at $100 million.[1]

The Power of Exchange

Jesus often taught His disciples using parables. In the following lesson, He likens the Kingdom of God to a man who searches for a great treasure, a pearl of immense value.

> *Again, the kingdom of heaven is like a merchant seeking beautiful pearls, who, when he had found one pearl of great price, went and sold all that he had and bought it* (Matthew 13:45-46).

For starters, I am acutely aware of the various interpretations surrounding this parable. However, I want to project a different thought about this story that will help us see the value of God's glory and what it takes to attain it.

Evidently the merchant in the parable heard there were a few rare pearls that existed somewhere in the world. Where? He didn't exactly know, but he knew they existed. His travels took him far and wide, from city to city, village to village hoping to find at least one of these exquisite pearls of infinite value.

It is unknown how long he searched for this elusive gem—how and where he discovered the pearl will remain a mystery, but he did find it. Undoubtedly, when he saw the pearl for the first time he was mesmerized, arrested by its majestic beauty; to him there was nothing else like it in the world. To some it was nothing more than hardened calcium, to others a meaningless token, but to him it was simply ravishing—what he longed for his whole life.

He asked the owner how much it would cost to buy the pearl. The answer was more than he imagined. It was expensive, a great price, well beyond the money he had on his person and even in his savings account. This shocking news didn't deter him in the least.

He took another look at the gorgeous pearl and thought, *This is worth everything I own, no price is too much to pay.* He was determined to purchase the pearl. He traveled home without the pearl. However, the text implies the man drained all of the money he had in his bank account, but it wasn't enough. He then sold all that he had. ALL. Everything. He liquidated every possession he owned. *"…he…went and sold all that he had and bought it"* (Matthew 13:46).

Think for a moment the impact this pearl had on him. The pearl was so beautiful, elusive, unique and perfect that he was willing to part with everything that belonged to him in order to possess it for himself. The text doesn't say it, but it is possible that when he returned home he dragged all of his possessions into the front yard and posted a For Sale sign.

It is worth repeating, don't miss it, *"…he…sold all that he had and bought it."* All means all. He sold his camel, his home, and even all of the furniture inside the house, including his bed, the sheets on the bed, his field, his farming equipment, his tools, his shovel, his business, his animals, his family heirlooms, his children's possessions, their toys, their pets, his wife's clothes, her jewelry, his garments, all of it. Nothing was spared. For what? This one pearl.

No doubt when someone came to purchase his couch they asked, "Why are you selling your couch?" Perhaps he would tell the story, "Well, there is this really stunning pearl that I must possess and I'm selling all my stuff to get it." Some would look at him and say, "Oh really? You're giving up your mattress for a pendant?" Of course they said it with a half-smile and a gentle nod of the head as they gave him the money.

I'm sure some laughed and mocked while others doubted and perhaps questioned his mental stability. Then there is his family, wife and children. I wonder what they thought as their dad took their special toys and trinkets to the curb to sell to the highest bidder. I am sure they didn't fully understand. It didn't matter, he wanted the pearl; to him it was the greatest treasure on earth. Its value was inestimable and worth every sacrifice necessary to obtain it. Without question those closest to him were understandably nervous, his bankers, neighbors, in-laws, and his friends.

He bought it!

I don't believe this was an emotional purchase. It was premeditated. The text reveals he was searching for it, and I believe he had decided long before he found it that he would do whatever it took to own a pearl like this. In this man's eyes the "great price" he paid for the pearl was very small compared to the true value of the pearl.

Let's take a close look at him for a minute. He has nothing left—no home, no shoes, no clothes, just a pearl in his hands. He holds it and looks at it. He's happy. Yet, he is now homeless, he has no furniture, no bed to sleep on, but he is completely satisfied, for he owns the one thing he longed for, the pearl.

The Lord doesn't shame the man but highlights his willingness to do whatever was necessary to attain the pearl. This leads me to the obvious question: How bad do you want His glory on your life and ministry?

Before you answer, think about it. You first must count the cost to acquire His glory, because there is a cost, it isn't free. His grace is free, but His glory is not.

How much, you ask? The glory of God will cost you everything. Are you willing to sell all that you have for the pearl? Are you willing to relinquish everything in order to hold it in your hand? There is no shortcut. No one can give it to you. The price must be paid individually and it is expensive, very expensive.

Some will look at the pearl, the glory, and admire its beauty and all of its wonder, but decide the price is too high. They will mutter, "I can't afford it." Others will cry out, "Isn't there another way?" When they hear the answer "no," they will quietly walk away just like the rich young ruler did when he inquired about eternal life and Jesus said, *"Sell all that you have...and come, follow Me"* (Luke 18:22). He wanted eternal life but the price was more than he was willing to pay. He was a businessman and acquainted with the law of exchange; he knew it would cost him something, but never thought it would cost him everything. Sadly, the rich young ruler walked away from the greatest offer of his lifetime (see Luke 18:18-23).

Rest assured God will test your resolve, endurance, and your sincerity. He always does. His glory is like a pearl of great price and will not give it to people and churches that are not willing to pay the price to have it. He will not lower the price to attain it— it is too precious.

Let me implore you to do whatever you have to do, pay whatever price you have to pay for His glory. Don't simply be an observer and admirer—be a possessor. And when you possess the pearl of great value, don't hide it under your bed for ten years, or even ten minutes. Share it with the world! You and those around you will be glad you did.

ENDNOTE

1. Roberta Naas, "This $100 Million Pearl Is the Largest and Most Expensive in the World," Forbes, August 23, 2016 https://www .forbes.com/sites/robertanaas/2016/08/23/100-million-pearl -hidden-under-bed-sets-world-record-as-largest-most-expensive -pearl-in-the-world/#74d57e7c79b0; accessed May 18, 2020.

15

FROM PRISONER TO PREACHER

"The touch of God is marked by tears, weeping, it comes when that last barrier is down and you surrender yourself."
—DAVID WILKERSON

I saw him out of the corner of my eye, Robert is his name; he was hiding behind the other prisoners. Yep, trying to hide; however, it's hard to hide that much humanity.

No, I wasn't in a prison ministering to inmates. I was at Restoration Fire Ministries with Pastor Craig and Sue Ann Toney. I was invited to Sulphur Springs to bring the North Georgia Revival to this small East Texas town.

I know what you are thinking, *How did a group of prisoners end up at a church service?* Great question. One month earlier I was in this same church when the glory of God descended as we baptized more than 100 people. Unbelievable miracles, restoration, deliverances, and salvations occurred right before our eyes. The county judge and the local jail warden had attended the Friday and Saturday night services. They concluded it would be a great idea to bus a small group of inmates to the revival the following month.

This leads me back to Robert, who confessed later that he attended the revival service only for the free pizza. He was doing his best to be invisible, but there were two considerable issues that presented a problem for Robert: He's a large man weighing 275 pounds; and second, God knew exactly where he was and the Lord wanted to meet with him.

Robert carefully kept his eye on many of his friends who were in line to be baptized. He witnessed how each prisoner who entered the water was visibly shaken by the power of God. This made Robert all the more nervous.

I glanced to my right and I saw him, big Robert, and the Lord said to me, "Call him to come be baptized." I was a little nervous because he was so big, but I obeyed and said, "Hey you." I pointed right at him. He was completely startled and stood still as if he was frozen in place. I then again said, "Hey you." He pointed at himself to clarify it was him I was addressing. I said, "Yes, you. God wants you to come get in the water."

He hesitated at first as if trying to figure everything out. Then it happened. He began slowly and cautiously walking toward the baptismal tank. Every step was measured. God was in the room and everyone knew it. He later testified that as he walked toward the baptistery, his feet felt like they were on fire.

After what seemed an eternity, Robert finally reached the tank. He stopped and waited at the edge of the pool; I could see that his mind was working and thoughts were flashing through his brain, analyzing the severity of this moment. Before descending into the water, he took a deep breath as if he knew the life he once lived was coming to an end and the life he longed for was one water burial away.

Robert was a bad man—a very bad, angry man. Violence was a way of life for him. He had stabbed and even killed people. In a private meeting he confessed to me that he would get turned on watching people bleed out after he beat up or stabbed them. It was exhilarating for him to watch people in pain.

Also, big Robert was a member of the Aryan Nations, an anti-Semitic, white supremacist, terrorist organization. He hated black people. While in prison he had proven his trustworthiness to the Aryan Nations hierarchy, so he advanced through the ranks and was given more authority and responsibility within the organization. He became so powerful and influential that even while in solitary confinement he controlled Aryan Nations gang activity in four other state prisons. Aryans in other states, one over a thousand miles away, would follow his orders. Now, he found himself at the entrance of a baptistery about to have an encounter with Jesus.

Robert took a step forward. I will never forget when his right foot made contact with the water, he spread his arms like an eagle in mid-flight as far as he could, looked upward with tears running down his face and said, "I've always wanted something like this."

We were in no hurry, we let him take his time; there was no need to rush the moment as God was working on him. God's arm was reaching out to him from the midst of the water...inviting Robert to take hold of His hand.

The bystanders were mesmerized as before he was immersed, this robust man with both feet firmly planted, placed both hands over his face and wept like a baby. God was melting big Robert right before our eyes. God's overwhelming love, conviction, and power settled on him. We watched Heaven and all of its glory come upon a very wicked man.

It took two grown men to help submerge him to be baptized. Honestly, I didn't think the tank would hold him—it almost didn't. Two inches of water splashed over the edge of the tank onto the sanctuary floor when he was fully immersed.

While under the water, the Lord met Robert with a ferociousness that was completely unexpected. I have witnessed thousands of baptisms, but I will never forget this one. Robert had a supernatural encounter with Jesus that rocked him to the core.

When Robert came up for air he immediately placed his hands on his face again and began to cry, and we heard him whisper, "Precious, precious, precious."

In between the sobbing I asked Robert why he was saying, "Precious."

He replied, "When I was in the water, I saw Jesus' face—and it was precious!"

There was an immediate transformation right there in that tank. Jesus met Robert and he became a new man. God took a violent, hate-filled man and in one moment in the water delivered him from all the anger, hatred, and drugs that ruled his life.

Robert's conversion was so authentic and life changing that he quickly was looked upon by the other inmates as their spiritual leader and pastor. The most remarkable part of the story is that he became best friends with Melroy. Melroy is a African American man and the two of them together pastor the jail. They love each other as if flesh and blood brothers.

Only God can take a violent Aryan Nations gang member and touch his heart so deeply that he no longer hates anyone—now he loves everyone.

Oh, for the record, the prisoners no longer call him Robert, they call him "Precious."

Part Three

FROM LUKEWARM TO RED HOT

16

WE DIMMED
HIS LIGHT

*"The less Holy Spirit we have, the more cake and
coffee we need to keep the church going."*
—REINHARD BONNKE

I t seems we have done something to the gospel. We touched
it. It's different. Its DNA has been altered. It is no longer
hard-core.

I recently spoke to a significant ministry leader who pastors
eight church campuses and he described what happened this way,
"We have brought the culture to the Bible, rather than taking the
Word to the culture." This isn't a play on words, there is depth to
the statement.

How did this altered gospel happen?

A few decades ago, church growth analysts conducted research to find out why church attendance and interest in God was declining. They asked the unchurched what they didn't like about religion, church, and God.

The research was copious, well done, and even necessary. The culture spoke clearly and revealed to us what they did and didn't like about church and how we did it. The information gathered from the unbelieving community was eye-opening. And because we loved the unsaved, we adopted a new philosophical and theological approach to ministry, hoping to attract unbelievers.

The "community" asked for four things:

1. Services would be positive and uplifting
2. Shorten the length of the worship service
3. Provide a dynamic and entertaining children's ministry
4. No weird stuff (charismatic demonstrations causing people to feel uncomfortable)

This general list intentionally or unintentionally became the new framework for growing a culturally relevant church. It caused many pastors to evaluate their effectiveness; and as a result, some churches radically changed how they did church. Not only did many of their methods change, but in some cases so did their theology. Great efforts were made to remove every possible obstacle so unbelievers and seekers could comfortably and authentically encounter the Lord.

Not to oversimplify the issue, but the Church revamped its approach in order to attract a post-Christian society back to church.

Please hear my heart. This is not a judgment or a tired rant, but an observation.

In complying to the four responses, leaders took the edge off the gospel. A significant amount of potency of the gospel was removed for the sake of societal relevancy. The intention was good; the outcome pastors wanted was noble because they wanted more people to hear the gospel and eventually be won to Christ. However in order to do this, many felt it was necessary to tone things down a little—yes, that even meant they would not talk about the "difficult" passages in the Bible.

Again, the motive was to bring people in to have a born-again experience, and it seemed that meant removing as many potential stumbling blocks as possible. In doing so, many limited (intentionally or unintentionally), underemphasized, or discouraged the role, manifestation, or expression of the Holy Spirit in our services.

It appears that many leaders were and are still trying to keep something unusual from happening that may embarrass God or their attenders, perhaps both. It is not that they don't believe in the Holy Spirit, they do; they don't want the Holy Spirit and how people respond to the Holy Spirit to embarrass them or scare off people they are trying to reach.

Many people have a hard time following the reasoning behind why they do church this way, but let me explain why some chose this pathway of ministry. If you are hosting a first-time guest in your home for dinner and conversation, naturally you want to make a lasting positive impression, hoping a friendship develops. But, you have a child prone to very expressive behavior and at any given moment says whatever he or she is thinking. Most of the time it is wonderful, but there have been other times when you have been mortified by what and when it was said. It made you and your guest very uncomfortable.

Therefore, since many parents know what could potentially happen, they purposely limit the child's exposure and conversation to their potential new friends. It's not that you don't love your child, but you don't want to have an awkward moment if you can prevent it.

Some churches know this can happen in their services when the Holy Spirit is involved—so the agenda is strictly scripted. Very little time is allowed for spontaneity and visible expressions. Leaders control the moments in the service and everyone knows what is allowed and not allowed.

However, to satisfy the demand from some in their congregation who want the Holy Spirit to move with freedom, some churches have allocated a special service once a month or once a quarter that gives the Holy Spirit an outlet to do what He wants to do. This is usually set in place to satisfy the group of congregants who believe there is more and want more.

Honestly, it's like the Holy Spirit has been put away or locked up—and to see Him, you come by during visiting hours. If you want to see and experience Him, here is the time when He will be available. Afterward, He goes back into His designated place of obscurity.

But let me remind us all that God birthed the Church with chaotic exploits. If at any time God should have wanted to be "sensitive to the unchurched," it would have been at the start. Naturally speaking, common (human) sense would not have made the beginning of this new movement so offensive and outrageous.

Yet in Acts 2 when the Holy Spirit fell on the disciples in the upper room, the encounter was highly unusual and led to an extravagant display of what some in our day would call weird and counterproductive. Not surprisingly, three out of the five responses to the coming and manifestation of the Holy Spirit was negative. It is worth noting that God didn't have a problem with the Holy Spirit, and in short order three thousand people were saved and added to the Church. They were born again in the midst of highly unusual displays of God's Spirit.

Open the Door for Him

The next quote seems to have been the modus operandi for a couple of decades, "When people come to worship with us, let's give them a high-quality experience and eliminate any potential moments that may scare or make our guests feel uncomfortable." On top of that, so not to offend anyone or run anyone off, it became important to avoid certain issues like sin, repentance, holiness, etc. The strategy was obvious—keep everything positive, uplifting, and encouraging.

As a result, the "sermons" became "messages" and were more about how to have a happy, successful, fulfilling life while here on earth. There is nothing inherently wrong with this, but that became the steady diet for many.

Pastors backed off and we pulled away from the difficult truths of the Bible. Rather, we decided to preach mainly positive, inspiring messages. Pastors started seeing themselves more as life coaches than pastors; therefore, they for the most part avoided the hard messages dealing with correction, reproof, and purity. Collectively, they offered an amazing spiritual diet of "cookies and cream" from the pulpits and created a generation of spiritual diabetics addicted to spiritual sugar and avoiding the strong meat of the Word.

All of this seems logical to the natural mind, but it has created an unprepared Church ill-prepared to face the challenges of our broken society.

Toys "R" Us Preachers

Not long ago a preacher addressing a large denomination convention made these scathing indictments about the modern-day pastor, "You don't want nothing but toys. You are a Toys "R" Us preacher. You are the candy man because the candy man makes the world taste good. You make the world taste good. You won't tell them the truth because you want the numbers. You know who you are. You are Bishop Nimrod pastoring a Babylonian church with a Walmart marketing system that cuts the price to keep the people coming."

Charles Finney, in 1875, loudly declared for the world to hear the importance of pastors preaching the truth. He said:

Brethren, our preaching will bear its legitimate fruits. If immorality prevails in the land, the fault is ours in a great degree. If there is a decay of conscience, the pulpit is responsible for it. If the public press lacks moral discrimination, the pulpit is responsible for it. If the church is degenerate and worldly, the pulpit is responsible for it. If the world loses its interest in religion, the pulpit is responsible for it. If Satan rules in our halls of legislation, the pulpit is responsible for it. If our politics become so corrupt that the very foundations of our government are ready to fall away, the pulpit is responsible for it. Let us not ignore this fact, my dear brethren; but let us lay it to heart, and be thoroughly awake to our responsibility in respect to the morals of this nation.[1]

A.W. Tozer (1897-1963) offered a stern warning to not only the pastors and church leaders of his generation, but to all who would come after him. He said:

Save me from the curse that lies dark across the modern clergy: the curse of compromise, of imitation, of professionalism. Save me from the error of judging a church by its size, its popularity or the amount of its yearly offering. Help me to remember that I am a prophet—not a promoter, not a religious manager, but a prophet. Let me never become a slave to crowds. Heal my soul of carnal ambitions and deliver me from the itch of publicity. Save me from bondage to things. Let me not waste my days puttering around the house. Lay Thy terror upon me, O God, and drive me to the place of prayer where I may wrestle with principalities and powers and the rulers of the darkness of this world. Deliver me from overeating and late sleeping. Teach me self-discipline that I may be a good soldier of Jesus Christ.[2]

John Wesley, who led a revival movement known as Methodism, wrote a letter addressing the wayward state of many clergy of his time. Here is the letter in part that he wrote to Alexander Mather dated August 6, 1777:

> No, Aleck, no! The danger of ruin to Methodism does not lie here. It springs from quite a different quarter. Our preachers, many of them are fallen. They are not spiritual. They are not alive to God. They are soft, enervated fearful of shame, toil, hardship. They have not the spirit which God gave to Thomas Lee at Pateley Bridge or to you at Boston. Give me one hundred preachers who fear nothing but sin and desire nothing but God, and I care not a straw whether they be clergymen or laymen, they alone will shake the gates off hell and set up the kingdom of heaven upon earth.[3]

Today we are reaping seismic results due to the spirit of accommodation that invaded our pulpits years ago. The result? I strongly believe the overall church is more diluted of power than ever before.

We lost the culture when we stopped preaching the controversial and sometimes uncomfortable, offensive gospel. Alexis de Tocqueville, author of Democracy in America in the early 1800s, is credited with the following analysis of the American pulpit:

> I looked throughout America to find where her greatness originated. I looked for it in her harbors and on her

shorelines, in her fertile fields and boundless prairies, and in her gold mines and vast world commerce, but it was not there. It was not until I went to the churches of America and heard her pulpits aflame with righteousness did I understand the secret of her success. America is great because she is good, and if America ceases to be good, America will cease to be great.

Our pulpits must be baptized with the fire of the Holy Spirit; and once again with love and conviction we have to preach the other side of the gospel. You know the part, where Jesus commands us to deny yourself, and take up your cross daily, and follow Him (see Luke 9:23). While we are at it, let's include Paul's statements to his son-in-the-faith Timothy, *"Let everyone who names the name of Christ depart from iniquity"* (2 Timothy 2:19). And where Paul wrote, *"And have no fellowship with the unfruitful works of darkness..."* (Ephesians 5:11).

I agree that over time methods change, they must—but perhaps we have made the method more important than the message. We are now realizing one big mistake we made was attempting to bring the culture to the Bible. In other words, trying to appease the culture by presenting scriptural talks that help improve their lives without calling them to repentance, holiness, and a total surrendering to the lordship of Christ.

Thankfully, pastors everywhere are now shifting away from this cookies and cream approach. Why? It hasn't produced the heart and lifestyle change we were longing for. We are going back and adopting Jesus' model of ministry. He presented the message of the gospel and declared that in order to partake you must adjust to it. His expectations and demands never wavered—and they shouldn't for us as well.

A new breed of pastors is emerging in this hour, bold men and women who will unapologetically preach the whole message of Jesus. This new breed will capture the heart of the Father and lay their lives down for His sake.

ENDNOTES

1. Charles Finney was a leader of the Second Great Awakening. This quote is from a sermon titled, "The Decay of Conscience", issuing a warning to all Americans, especially believers.
2. This was part of A.W. Tozer's private prayer after his ordination at the age of 23.
3. Wesley Center Online; http://wesley.nnu.edu/john-wesley/the -letters-of-john-wesley/wesleys-letters-1777; accessed May 18, 2020.

17

JUDGMENT IS COMING...MAYBE

"The fate of America is in the hands of the Church, oh to God that our pulpits would understand the gravity of this hour."
—TODD SMITH

Throughout the years many in the Church have said that God will judge the United States because of its sin. I am not disagreeing with that statement nor am I minimizing it, for it is true. However, in my opinion, currently, the biggest threat to our society is not sinners doing what sinners do. People are born with a fallen nature that impulsively rebels against God. For example, you don't have to teach a child to steal or lie, it is part of our nature. Therefore sinners will sin and at times it will be an ugly mess—people are hurt, killed, lives shattered, families ruined, injustices everywhere.

I do believe that the sin of this nation and every nation is ever-present before the Lord and He is not pleased with what He sees. History confirms God has pronounced devastating judgments on nations and people groups who rebelled against Him—and with one stroke of His hand He has taken away kings and their kingdoms. God has brought many influential nations to a humiliating end because of their wickedness and unwillingness to walk in His ways.

Is the United States next? Will God judge our land?

The following is a small reflection of our national sins; it is not exhaustive, but it is a sweeping list of deeds that our nation condones and/or participates in:

- Abortion
- Racism
- Violence
- Murder
- Thievery
- Mind-altering drug use
- Extortion
- Governmental and political corruption
- Sexual perversion
- Removal of God from public life; for example, removing prayer from school and the Ten Commandments from public buildings
- Human trafficking

- LGBQT advancement

Again, this is a small sampling, but nonetheless a good representation of the state of our nation that has little to zero fear of God.

In light of everything on this list, I would like to put things in perspective and softly address an issue that could be misinterpreted and misunderstood.

In my opinion, the biggest threat to our nation and most dangerous segment in and to our society is not the terrorists who live among us, nor is it the hideous abortion industry as violent, murderous, and satanic as that is. In fact, racism, as repulsive and dehumanizing as it is, is not our biggest problem, nor is the corruption in government as dreadful and embarrassing as it may be. Furthermore, I don't believe that pulling the Bible and prayer out of schools or the removal of the Ten Commandments from the public buildings as painful as it was to witness will be responsible for our nations demise, nor our nation's involvement in the destructive human trafficking industry. I don't even believe the LGBQT community and its straightforward agenda and perversion will solely be responsible for bringing this nation under the judgment of God.

Again, I am not minimizing nor neutralizing the national and personal atrocities previously mentioned. However, I want to propose to you the most crippling element in our country, an embedded segment of our society that has been here from the inception of our great land. I dare say this group at large is having an unintentional negative impact on our culture and nation.

You ask, "Who is this group?" Hang on, because it may surprise you.

It is a fearful, unmotivated, consumer-based, sleeping, convenience-seeking, untrained, offended, carnal, lukewarm, lazy, entitled, unholy, and prayerless Church.

Don't get offended and become angry, but by and large the Church in general has had *"a form of godliness but denying its power"* (2 Timothy 3:5). I understand not all believers fall in this category, but way too many do and it is having a devastating impact on our country.

It is difficult to disagree with the idea that America has drifted into deeper levels of darkness because the Church has not stood her ground and/or manifested the power of the Kingdom of God. We have built bigger buildings while losing more territory to the kingdom of darkness. Our bank accounts have increased but our influence has become minimal.

In general, the Church's inactivity has yielded considerable ground to the enemy. For the most part we, the worldwide Church, have sat quietly on the sidelines as the very foundation of our Republic, which was founded on Judeo-Christian values, has been eroding before our eyes.

The moral decency and common civility we once knew has been replaced by self-promotion, vitriol, and vulgarity of the rawest kind. Our core values have been highjacked by special interest groups who unashamedly promote an aggressive godless agenda. How did this happen? It was a slow fade that took decades to accomplish.

For example, collectively the Church watched as one woman, Norma McCorvey,[1] aka Jane Roe, changed the nation's stance about abortion, which has subsequently caused the death of more than sixty million unborn children. She took a stand to be able to control her reproductive rights, and in 1973 the U.S. Supreme Court ruled that during the first trimester of pregnancy a woman had the right to abort the child.

Where were the nation's churches? Honestly, ask the question. At that time, 211 million people lived in the United States and nearly 90 percent of the population identified themselves as Christian. Where were the pastors, prophets, evangelists, apostles, and teachers? Where were the intercessors? The elders? Board members? Laity?

Here is another example of our passive inactivity. In 1958, one highly motivated parent, Steven Engel, along with a small group of parents, promoted the removal of this simple prayer from our public schools, "Almighty God, we acknowledge our dependence on Thee, and beg Thy blessings upon us, our teachers, and our country." The United States Supreme Court ruled the practice unconstitutional. Again, the questions must be asked and answered: Where were the churches? Where were the protests, the boycotts? Were churches unconcerned, disinterested? How did this happen when so many in society proclaimed to be Christians?

My intention is not to denigrate the Church, nor am I bashing our wonderful country. I love the Church and our nation. Furthermore, I believe God loves our country and has been very patient with us. His goal is not to destroy us but to save us and use us for His glory.

Oprah Winfrey reacted to two mass shootings in August 2019 this way, "We will be lost until America finds the moral center churches used to provide."

If the Church, even if it is just a small segment within, captured and understood its purpose and potential, plus wholeheartedly repented and prayed, the glory of God could be released upon our land. We cannot afford the void left in our society by a carnal Church. She must arise and adorn herself with His glory and save the nation. The Church is the only hope for the world, as I heard it said once, "The Church is plan A—and there isn't a plan B."

I stand on solid ground when I say, if we get the Church right, then everything else will fall into place. For example, homes will get right, communities will get right, schools will get right, government will get right, society will get right.

It's not only necessary to get the right politicians in place—we need the right preachers in place as well. Ones who totally understand the severity of this hour and the depravity of our collective condition. Preachers who are not interested in just building audiences and ministries, but in remaking America.

All of creation eagerly waits for the full manifestation of the children of God. The world is longing for the unveiling of the Church; she must come forth. We call her to her rightful place.

For the creation waits in eager expectation for the children of God to be revealed (Romans 8:19 NIV).

Just Ten Will Do

As previously stated, the evil of a nation is ever-present before the Lord. The sins of a people have a devastating effect not only on those involved, but others as well. For example, the wickedness of Sodom and Gomorrah was so grievous that the Lord heard the outcry from the people (Genesis 18:20-21).

The lifestyles and behaviors of the inhabitants of the city were so extreme God commissioned two angels to conduct an investigation. He wanted an eyewitness report on exactly what was taking place. The angels found the city just as God had heard, steeped in ghastly behaviors and unimaginable sin. The society was unashamed and fully depraved.

Meanwhile, God had a pointed conversation with Abraham. He notified Abraham that He was going to bring terrible judgment against the city. Abraham pleaded for God to show mercy and asked Him to spare the people. God agreed to forfeit the judgment if He could find fifty righteous people.

God searched the city and couldn't find fifty righteous people. So Abraham approached God and wanted to renegotiate the terms. He was able to convince God into lowering the number of righteous people by five. Once again, God searched the city streets, places of worship, and the homes of the people of Sodom and Gomorrah in hopes of finding forty-five righteous individuals—but once again He found none.

This back and forth went on until God agreed to spare the people if He could find ten righteous people.

Once again, God searched everywhere, but sadly couldn't find the ten He needed to postpone His judgment. You probably know the rest of the story—judgment came and all were destroyed.

God has sent us two definitive messages. One, His desire is to save and not to destroy. Second, and often times overlooked, God's people could have prevented the devastating judgment that fell upon the city. Note, not the sinners, but the righteous had the power to divert disaster.

If nations crumble, it will not be the fault of sinners alone. It will be direct result of the saints who sat by and did little to nothing to stop the moral decline.

Not to oversimplify the issue, but if a nation morally collapses and falls into the judgment of God, these three reasons will play a part:

- First, the Church not praying fervently and interceding with broken hearts over the condition of the people they live among.
- Second, God's people neglecting to walk in their God-given Kingdom authority that demonstrates the love and goodness of God.
- Third, failure of believers to manifest the authentic Christian life by living separated and holy and above reproach before the Lord and the people they desperately were commissioned to reach.

The sad epitaph of many will be: "They lived among them and became like them." May we not be like Lot and his children who became just like their culture (Genesis 19). God was willing to spare a perverted, outrageously depraved people if He could find ten righteous ones within the city (Genesis 18:32).

Can God find ten in your city?

ENDNOTE

1. In 1995, McCorvey became involved in Operation Rescue, a pro-life organization, and she aggressively campaigned against abortion. She wrote two memoirs chronicling her infamous life, *I Am Roe* and *Won by Love*. https://www.britannica.com/biography/Norma-McCorvey; accessed May 18, 2020.

18

BUILD ME AN ARMY

"Jesus didn't command us to pray for the sick.
He commanded us to heal them."
—BILL JOHNSON

The Great Commission was given to every child of God, all of it.

And Jesus came and spoke to them, saying, "All author-
ity has been given to Me in heaven and on earth. Go
*therefore and **make disciples** of all the nations, **baptiz-***
***ing** them in the name of the Father and of the Son and of*
*the Holy Spirit, **teaching** them to observe all things that*
I have commanded you; and lo, I am with you always,
even to the end of the age." Amen (Matthew 28:18-20).

There isn't one phrase that doesn't apply to each believer. However, most believers are unable to perform any one of the assignments given by Jesus. If you think I have overgeneralized and drawn an unfair conclusion, ask fellow believers to share with you the gospel plan of salvation. If that is not enough proof, ask them to go and pray and lay hands on your sick neighbor. Encourage them to share with you how they would approach and minister to someone who is demonized. Watch their response, hear their fears as they legitimately share why they don't feel qualified for such assignments.

A couple of years ago I clearly heard the Lord speak to me, "Todd, do not build Me a church full of attenders—build Me an army I can use."

His statement exploded in my spirit! His word was not optional to me, it wasn't a suggestion—it was a mandate. God sees life different from how we see it. He knows what is directly ahead and what the Church is about to go through. His instruction to me was clear, and I knew He was serious. The Church must become ready.

To fulfill God's desire of building Him an army, I had to change how we "did" church. This wasn't easy. No question, we were somewhat successful in people attending our worship service; and while there we encouraged them to keep moving forward and to be the best Christians they could be.

However, our sermons and small groups were mostly about helping my members fulfill their destiny, making them more successful in life, and overall "better" people—sadly, not so much about making them usable for the Lord.

> *Therefore if anyone cleanses himself from the latter,*
> *he will be a vessel for honor, sanctified and useful for*
> *the Master, prepared for every good work* (2 Timothy
> 2:21).

I don't want you to take this wrong way, but the fact is, far too many believers are not usable to Jesus. Do these Christians love Jesus? Absolutely, amazingly so. However, they are not equipped for whatever reason(s) to assist Jesus in expanding the Kingdom of God.

Regretfully, a good many Christians cannot lead someone to Christ, exercise their authority over demons, and/or lay hands on the sick and see them recover. Embarrassingly, I say this with confidence because the majority of my people could not perform those tasks. They simply weren't usable, and it was my fault.

My ministry past, perhaps your ministry as well, had a church culture that developed Christians into becoming good listeners, attenders, and givers, but was weak in equipping them for the work of the ministry (Ephesians 4:11). Unfortunately, like me, pastors have been conditioned and programmed to gage our effectiveness in ministry based on how many people show up for one of our weekend services. Subsequently, this has led us to believe that God is pleased and we are doing all He has asked us to do. I rejoice in the fact that people want to attend our worship services, but God requires more from His leaders than gathering a crowd. I quickly realized God was not impressed with the metrics I employed to measure my ministry success.

The shift of focus didn't come easy for our church. We took a long and extensive look at how effective we were in preparing people to do the work of the ministry. We were not pleased with the findings and realized we needed to do a better job at training our people for Kingdom advancement.

In the days and months that followed, our assignment was crystal clear, "Make My people usable to Me."

We methodically positioned our people to be usable to the Lord, even outside of the church setting. Our goal wasn't to simply teach people to persevere and survive life, but develop them into someone God could use in the marketplace.

I didn't realize it at the time, but the Lord was posturing us to be able to host His presence and be the hub of an international movement, the North Georgia Revival. Our commitment to make our church family usable was a key factor that attracted His attention and ultimately His glory.

"How Many?"

I am strongly convinced that when I stand before Him on my going home day, He will never ask me, "How many attended your church? How many services do you have?" Or, "How many campuses do you have?" But I do believe, as a pastor and leader of His flock, He will want to know how successful I was in making the people He entrusted to me usable for Him.

Part Four

USEFUL AND
USED BY GOD

19

I'M AFRAID OF THE DARK

"The greater the anointing; then greater the isolation."
—Pat Schatzline

I love the story of the little boy who was petrified of the dark.

One evening his mother asked him to go out to the back porch and bring her the broom. The little boy said, "Mama, please don't make me go out there. It's dark and you know I'm scared of the dark."

His mother smiled at him and said reassuringly, "There's no need to be afraid of the dark. Jesus is out there and He'll look after you and protect you."

The little boy seemed unsure and said, "Are you sure Jesus is out there?"

The mother said, "Yes, I'm sure. Jesus is everywhere and is always there and ready to help when you're in need."

The boy thought for a moment, then he went to the back door and opened it a tiny bit. He looked out into the darkness and called out, "Jesus, if you're out there, please hand me the broom."

Why are we afraid of the dark? Is it because we can't see our surroundings? Do we feel vulnerable and unprotected? Have you noticed your heart rate increases and your pace quickens when walking through a dark place? Our instinct is to avoid the dark and seek the light. We don't want any part of the dark, and we go to great lengths to eliminate it. Why? Perhaps it's because we don't know what lurks in the shadows.

In 1890, the United States had approximately 175,000 electric streetlights to help keep our neighborhoods safe. Today, there are more than 26 million streetlights helping us make our way through the dark after the sun sets.

Clearly, one of the greatest inventions in the history of the world, especially for a child, was the nightlight. It's amazing that a little 2-watt lightbulb can instantly neutralize all perceived monsters hiding in the closet and underneath the bed.

Seriously, growing up we kids believed all kinds of spooky things existed in the dark. My mother and all the neighborhood moms must have thought so as well. I recall as if it were yesterday, as I would leave the house to go play outside my mom would always say, "Come home before dark."

Like most kids in the world we would play until the last morsel of light faded behind the trees. We tried to squeeze from the day as much playtime as possible. And on cue, right before dusk we heard mom after mom calling out children's names to come home. My mom and the others didn't want anything tragic to happen to us, so they demanded us to come inside.

Even though we have strong inhibitions about the dark, I have since learned that darkness is from God too. He created it.

> *For by Him all things were created that are in heaven and that are on earth, visible and invisible, whether thrones or dominions or principalities or powers. All things were created through Him and for Him* (Colossians 1:16).

In the beginning darkness was present before creation and has remained since creation. Darkness in its purest form is not evil or void of God, it simply has a deficiency of light. God is everywhere even in the dark.

> *Where can I go from Your Spirit? Or where can I flee from Your presence? If I ascend into heaven, You are there; If I make my bed in hell, behold, You are there. If I take the wings of the morning, and dwell in the utter-most parts of the sea, even there Your hand shall lead me, and Your right hand shall hold me. If I say, "Surely the darkness shall fall on me," even the night shall be light about me; indeed,* **the darkness shall not hide from You,** *but the night shines as the day;* **the darkness and the light are both alike to You** (Psalm 139:7-12).

You may not believe me, but darkness in a believer's life is good and necessary. You ask how I can say that when the Bible and society typically view darkness as evil, ungodly and/or ghostly? I say it because it's true. Not all darkness is bad. Some dark places are God-ordained and give God the necessary platform to display His most fascinating work. In many cases, darkness is the proving ground God uses to prepare us for battle.

Let me illustrate it for you with several examples from the Bible.

As I stated, in the beginning before God created the light, there was darkness—it covered the earth, it was everywhere. The book of Genesis reveals that God moved about and brought forth the earth while it was dark. Even after creating light, darkness remained.

The beloved Abraham was frustrated; many years had passed and even still he had no heir. God took him outside in the dark and said, *"I will make your descendants as numerous as the stars in the sky..."* (Genesis 26:4 NIV). This revelation could not have happened during the day.

Then there was Jacob who blatantly deceived his father and betrayed his brother. God found him after the sun had rested. And all night long, in the dark, Jacob wrestled with an Angel. Jacob cries out, "I will not let you go until you bless me." Jacob left the conflict with a limp, a much-needed blessing, and a brand-new name. The whole episode unfolded in the darkness and Jacob went from being known as the "Deceiver" to the "Prince with God" (Genesis 32:24-28).

Another example, the Children of Israel left Egypt not at noon but at night. When the Israelites were trapped between a large mountain, Pharaoh, the Egyptian army, and the Red Sea, God split the Red Sea, at night (Exodus 14:26-30). Plus, the manna that fell from the sky and fed the people of God descended while it was still dark (Numbers 11:9).

The New Testament reveals that Jesus met His Father multiple times in the dark. Some of Jesus' most powerful experiences happened in the deep belly of the night. No, not demonstrations of miracles, but pivot points in His ministry. For example, He prayed all night long before He chose His twelve disciples. He knew that the ones He chose would be closer to Him than all the others, and this small select group would ultimately be responsible for taking the gospel to the world (Luke 6:12). He needed the night.

During another pivotal moment in Jesus' life, He withdrew with three of his best friends and walked steadfastly into the dark to meet with His Father.

He asked Peter and two brothers to accompany Him to the garden. The sun had already lowered itself behind the gentle Galilean hills. The City of David and its glorious walls were in view. The fire lamps lit up the city that was robust with activity. It was one of Jesus' most difficult moments. He needed to be in a secluded place because He knew that in a few short hours He would be ruthlessly nailed to a cross.

The three who followed Him into the dark were tired and quickly fell asleep, but He lingered in the blackness and prayed. Again, in the darkness He met with His Father and Luke 22:43 declares that an angel strengthened Him. When? At night, in the dark.

The next day the disciples denied knowing Him, yet He persevered through the mock trial, scourging, humiliation, and brutality of the cross. Jesus knew the value of the dark.

As a student of revivals, I have observed and learned that darkness was and is the womb of all great moves of the Spirit. This is undeniable.

I admit, the dark is difficult, it truly is. No one likes the dark. We fight against it. However, I am convinced more than ever that God is in the dark and purposely draws us to meet Him there.

Surprisingly significant things happen in the dark. You find you. You discover your true self there. You also learn a few things about God that you can't find out anywhere else.

Furthermore, in the dark, and what happens there, allows and equips you to walk in another dimension of strength, wisdom, power and glory. Only here are spiritual authority and Kingdom power realized and activated. Jesus knew this truth and that is why He willingly walked into the darkness.

While we are running from the dark, perhaps, just maybe, God is nudging us there. The closed doors you are facing could be God escorting you into the night to encounter Him.

Isaiah the prophet said, *"I will give you the treasures of darkness and hidden riches of secret places, that you may know that I, the Lord, who call you by your name, am the God of Israel"* (Isaiah 45:3).

What a word picture, *"treasures of darkness...."* There are treasures in the dark! God beckons us to come into the room, shut the door and sit in the dark. Both personal and church revival is birthed in the dark. It has always been this way. There is no other way to have it.

We have to willingly walk into the dark, alone. Believe me, you will want to leave because it is so awkward and uncomfortable. Sitting alone in the dark is difficult at first, it's cold. I wasn't used to it. I was used to interaction, mobility, light.

I acknowledge that my life-changing encounter with God and the glory that is present at the North Georgia Revival was birthed in the dark. It came in isolation, lights out, all alone. It eventually became visible to the world on a Sunday night church service on February 11. However, it was brought forth at the altar of sacrifice in the dark.

> *Day after day I recall disconnecting from the world and forcing myself to walk into a dark room and simply agonize before the Lord. I was there to do business. I had come to the end of myself; I was desperate. I didn't go into the room to complain, or go over my list of woes, nor did I display my needs before Him—I simply wanted to dismantle my will before Him in the dark. I would drag myself up on the altar and beg God, "Please come and consume this flesh, kill it so You may be glorified." It was painful. I died a thousand deaths. I cried, I screamed, I yielded, and wailed unto exhaustion. At times my body would shake because I was so weary and worn out.*
>
> *It was in these moments, in the dark, when I wrestled with the embarrassing reality of the shallowness of my soul. I was made acutely aware of the profound emptiness that possessed me. The powerlessness of my ministry and fallowness of my own heart looked at me right in the eye. It wasn't pretty. Nothing was hidden from me and*

I didn't want it to be—I needed the truth. It was ugly but beautiful at the same time. The story of my life was being highlighted and exposed in the darkness.

Every day I went there, alone. Some days I dreaded it, other times I longed for it. There were times after being in the dark for an hour I would leave, believing I made no progress. I would walk away feeling nothing, no encounter, no dialogue, no change, zilch. I talked to Him, the conversation seemed to be so one-sided, it was as if Heaven was closed for the day. I wondered at times if He even cared. I would shout to Him, "I'm here! Where are You? Why won't You answer me? Here I am…use me!" I would wait on His answer, but nothing came.

God was draining me, breaking me. I was bleeding out slowly. I wanted intervention—He wanted depletion. He watched until I was at the utter end of myself.

Again, He was watching my pursuit, analyzing my heart to clearly see my motive. What was I truly pursuing? He wanted to know if I was after a blessing, another touch, or an authentic encounter with His face and heart. He was playing the quiet game. He simply sat and observed.

20

"I THINK I BUMPED INTO GOD"

"True revival is that divine moment when God bursts upon the scene and displays His glory."
—DEL FEHSENFELD JR.

Rabbi David Schneier and his lovely wife, Leslie, invited our team to share the story of how God was changing lives in the baptismal waters at the North Georgia Revival. They pastor Beth Hallel, a wonderful Messianic church in Birmingham, Alabama.

I will never forget what one sweet six-year-old girl said after her baptism. She had waited patiently in line and finally it was her turn. She looked nervous but determined. She had a porcelain look—beautiful and innocent. When she stepped into the water and descended the stairs, I asked her what we ask every person who enter the waters, "Why do you want to be baptized?" Her response, "I want to get closer to God." I smiled and was in complete agreement with her sweet desire to love Him more.

God must have been in agreement as well.

As we immersed her, she closed her eyes, took a deep breath, and held her nose. The water gently swooped over her entire body. All appeared normal until she came up out of the water. Immediately she started trembling. This wasn't completely unusual for I have seen this manifestation hundreds of times before. However, I was concerned that she was shaking due to the cool temperature of the water and I wanted her experience to be enjoyable.

When she climbed the stairs and exited the baptismal tank, she was still visibly shaking; everyone noticed it. I watched her closely. One of the assistants at the top of the steps asked her "Sweetheart, why are you shaking?" Her response was soft yet emphatic, "When I was underneath the water, I saw Jesus." She paused and then added, "And I think I bumped into God too."

This precious girl underneath the water, with her eyes closed, in the darkness saw Jesus! And at the same time, she said she "bumped into God too."

I'm convinced God does His best work in the dark. This presents a slight problem for us, because we love the light. The world we live in is a world of lights. We are drawn to the light.

Increasingly, people have adopted the spirit of the age and are crying out to be seen, noticed, liked, and followed. Instagram, Twitter, TikTok, and Facebook allow us to instantly highlight our lives for all the world to see. Our posts and tweets echo, "Take a look at what I'm doing. Watch me. Look how wonderful my life is."

Darkness is necessary! And some of us need darkness more than we need the light.

Poet May Sarton wrote, "Without darkness, nothing comes to birth, as without light, nothing flowers.

Think about the significance darkness has in the world. A diamond is forged in the deep recesses of the earth in total darkness. The pressure it experiences in complete obscurity is what makes it the most beautiful gem in the world.

A small embryo is conceived and for nine delicate months it abides in the darkness of the mother's womb. For three trimesters, forty weeks, the child will not see the light. In the dark God grows and matures the baby and prepares the child for the world.

A caterpillar enters a cocoon for a season of transformative agony and darkness; and in due time it emerges to spread its wings and paint the sky with its brilliant colors.

A seed produces fruit after being covered with the earth. While alone in the ground the seed dies and completely surrenders to the germination process. In a short while the seed becomes a plant and yields fruit for people to enjoy. But as long as a seed remains in the light, above ground, it cannot produce a harvest.

Jesus said, *"Most assuredly, I say to you, unless a grain of wheat falls into the ground and dies, it remains alone; but if it dies, it produces much grain"* (John 12:24).

If a seed isn't planted deep enough, it could dry up and wither due to the surface heat, and therefore cannot fulfill its assignment.

I love photography. Without a doubt it is my favorite form of art. A photograph captures an instant, a significant event, a person, or landscape of some sort and forever seals a precise second of time. Photographs allow us to look back at a season of our life and remember the moment. It is small window of history that would have been nothing more than a fading memory.

While most people today use digital cameras, many photographers still use film to capture images. The photos on film are taken in the light, but they are developed in the dark. While developing the film, if the film is exposed to light too soon, the photograph will be ruined. The film has to stay in the dark until the image is fully developed.

The dark has value!

A young boy was closely watching a moth struggling to free itself from its cocoon. To the boy the struggle seemed cruel and unnecessary. He felt sorry for the moth and wanted to help free it from its hardship.

The boy ran inside and retrieved a pair of his mother's scissors from a kitchen drawer. He proudly but cautiously walked over to the twitching moth to give what he thought was much-needed aid in order to release the moth from its entanglement.

As he gingerly snipped the last strand of webbing that clung to the moth, the boy fully anticipated it would fly away in its new-found freedom. However, the moth fell straightway to the ground below. The boy was puzzled and wondered why the moth was crawling around on the ground and not flying high in the sky.

What the boy didn't understand was that the moth's epic struggle to release itself from the cocoon was a necessary component of the maturation process. The fight for freedom was actually strengthening the moth by pushing blood to the tips of its wings so it could fly. The boy interrupted the process, thus he impeded the moth's growth. The moth never did take flight.

A baby that remains inside the womb forty weeks is called "full-term." A baby born before week thirty-seven is "premature." These "preemies," as they are referred to, are more susceptible to serious health problems than most full-term babies.

Doctors do everything they can to make sure the baby stays in the womb as long as possible. If the baby is birthed too soon, it could cause adverse health effects. Each day inside the womb is important for the child's development.

Throughout the ecosystems of life, God consistently affirms the value of the dark.

I recognize many are afraid of the dark and work feverishly to avoid it. But it is a good place; and while you are there, you are never alone. Let's not forget one of God's covenant names is Jehovah Shammah, which means God is there. You may not see Him, feel Him, or smell Him, but He is there.

David was ordained as a shepherd boy but was proven in dark places like the Cave of Adullam (1 Samuel 22:1).

Jesus, before He began His public ministry, spent forty days and nights in the wilderness separated from family and friends (Matthew 4:1-11).

After Paul's conversion, historians tell us he spent several years by himself being tutored by the Lord.

When God is preparing to use someone in the light, His first action is to escort that individual into the dark.

If you desire to be used by God, the dark cannot be avoided, it is part of His plan to prepare you to become usable to Him. Don't avoid, run from, neglect, or come out of the dark too soon. He is looking for an empty and completely drained vessel. There are many valuable lessons to be learned there. He will mold us and break us there; and just like a master craftsman, He will put us back together.

I have learned that the more broken you are, the more glory you can carry. I know that sounds unreasonable, but it's a Kingdom principle. The more shattered you are, the more usable you become.

Furthermore, what is developed in the dark room will shine in the light. It will be captivating and baffling to common people— they won't understand it. Like Moses, you will walk down the mountain and you will carry glory. You will walk differently, just as Jacob did as he wrestled with an Angel throughout the night and blazingly said, *"I will not let You go unless You bless me!"* (Genesis 32:26). Afterward, Jacob never walked the same, he emerged from the darkness with a gloriously noticeable limp.

Our time with God in the dark will alter our flesh, it must. The finger of God will make contact with you. Allow Him to chisel His brand upon you. Willingly, let Him mark you, scar you, disjoint you, burn you, and consume you.

We have turned the first page of the last chapter of time. In the dark God is preparing His warrior bride for this hour. I am convinced the end-time laborers will come out of the deep night; they will emerge suddenly, for they have been hidden until now. They will walk in an extraordinary level of authority and wisdom.

The full spectrum of God's power will be loosed upon the world. Men, women, teenagers, and even children will explode from the dark like a fireworks show and walk in unprecedented glory. The revealing of the sons and daughters whom the earth has been groaning for will finally come forth.

May I add caution? This new breed of believers will not be developed in the public eye, on our stages, or in our palaces of worship. No, they will come forth from the secret place, God's laboratory, the darkness.[1]

God keeps looking for you in the dark. It's your Bethel, your Mount Moriah, Garden of Gethsemane, your Cave of Adullam, your wilderness. Embrace the dark. Don't avoid it any longer. Give yourself to it. Walk into your closet and shut the door, close your eyes and seek God's face; who knows, you just may bump into Him.

> *I will give you the treasures of darkness. And hidden riches of secret places, that you may know that I, the Lord, who call you by your name, am the God of Israel* (Isaiah 45:3).

ENDNOTE

1. Of course I acknowledge that Jesus said, *"I am the light of the world. He who follows Me shall not walk in darkness, but have the light of life"* (John 8:12). And there are other Scriptures referring to Him as the "light," which is absolutely the truth. I hope this chapter opened another perspective of darkness for you and that you know now that God created both light and dark and He is with you in both.

21

DARING TO
DRAW NEAR

"Prayer is not a preparation for the battle; it is the battle!"
—LEONARD RAVENHILL

aria Robinson said it best, "Nobody can go back and
start a new beginning, but anyone can start today and
make a new ending."

Have you ever stopped at an unfamiliar street intersection and
you're not sure which way to turn? It's simple, right? Either you
turn right or left. You look both ways and evaluate, hoping that
something you see will help you make the right choice.

We are faced with multiple unfamiliar intersections throughout our lives. Which school should I attend? What should be my

career choice? Should I marry this person? What neighborhood will I live in? What school district do I want for my children? Do I take the job?

With every choice we make, there is a turn. For example, the choice turns us away from something and at the same time moves us toward something.

You ask how significant is the turn? It's everything.

He Turned and Looked

In a matter of a few seconds, in the midst of an unplanned moment, a man made a decision and with one pivot a shift took place that changed him, a nation, and even history. People hundreds of miles away who were unaware of the event would soon feel the full impact of a man who decided to turn and take a look.

Moses is 80 years old and standing on the back side of an unforgiving desert. It's his fortieth year of tending his father-in-law's sheep. By this time Moses has a routine, his job has become predictable and mundane. As a shepherd he is familiar with every inch of this rugged terrain as he has navigated the same hills for decades, looking for pockets of vegetation to feed his sheep.

God is in the perfect location. He knew Moses' traffic patterns and strategically organized a hopeful encounter, an opportunity for Moses to meet Him in a most unusual manner. God sets the trap, He ignites a bush and patiently waits for Moses to pass by.

In the midst of the ordinary, something a few yards off the beaten path catches Moses' attention—a bush, but not just any bush, a bush that was aglow with fire. Needless to say it intrigued him and caused him to take a second look. Moses probably had seen bushes on fire before, but this one was different. Typically a dry bush in the desert would burn out quickly, and in a matter of seconds the flames would turn the bush to ashes. But not this bush, it continued to burn.

God was closely watching how the faithful shepherd Moses would respond to the fiery bush. Moses turned (Exodus 3:3-4).

Here is what is so compelling about this story told in Exodus chapter 3. It's not that Moses saw the burning bush—no, it was that God spoke to Moses only after He saw that Moses turned toward the bush.

Think about it, this event was a well-orchestrated plan on God's part, a divine setup that involved a high level of risk. In what way? What if Moses didn't see the bush, what then? What if Moses would have decided to keep walking and not turn to take another look? Would God have spoken? Would God have called out Moses' name and say in essence, "Hey Moses, I'm over here!" I doubt it. God simply waited on his response; He was looking for the turn.

The text reveals it was only when God saw that Moses turned toward the fire that God spoke from the bush.

The implications are profound.

How we respond to Him determines what He does next. God is looking for the turn: *"If My people who are called by My name will humble themselves, and pray and seek My face, and turn..."* (2 Chronicles 7:14). There is something about the turn that causes God to say, "Yes! They responded."

> *Draw near to God* and *He will draw near to you.*
> *Cleanse your hands, you sinners; and purify your hearts,*
> *you double-minded* (James 4:8).

It's time to turn toward God. He will not force anything to happen in your life, there has to be the turn—it starts with you.

Here is a closing thought. How many of us are waiting on God to speak before we turn? Perhaps God is waiting on us to turn before He speaks.

Let's find the fire of God's glory, walk toward it, and then listen for His voice.

22

BROKEN AND NOT FOR SALE

"God never uses anyone greatly until He tests them deeply."
—A.W. TOZER

What do we usually do with broken things? Most people simply discard unusable items in the trash. However, some ingenious people try to profit from their junk by selling it at a yard sale.

I live in the south and on weekends, yard or garage sales are a way of life; signs are staked into the ground or stapled to a telephone pole advertising where and when the yard sale is taking place.

In the early days of our marriage, while a seminary student in Fort Worth, Texas, I needed a suit to wear to church. However like most seminary students, we were in the lower income bracket and didn't have the money to go buy a new one at the store. So we decided to buy a suit at an estate or yard sale. We traveled all over Fort Worth looking at yard sales hoping to find a suit. God answered my prayer—we happened upon an estate sale.

A woman's husband had recently passed and she was selling his belongings, including his clothes. I hit the jackpot. I walked into his closet and bam, there it was a blue pinstripe Christian Dior suit. It was a thousand-dollar suit, and I bought it for $25, can you believe it? Honestly, it felt a little creepy buying a dead guy's suit, but when I put that fine piece of clothing on, I immediately felt better. May God bless his soul.

Thank God for yard sales!

Did you know that yard sales are a multimillion dollar industry in the US? According to 2013 statistics, nearly 700,000 people each week visit yard sales in search of some serious bargains. On average, there are 165,000 yard sales each week that generate about $4.2 million in revenue for the yard sale hosts. According to those numbers, the average yard sale generates just under $26 in revenue per host, and the average price per item is 85 cents.[1]

What is usually sold in garage sales? Three things: items people no longer want, belongings they no longer use, and broken things. What some people deem to be unusable and ready to be discarded, others see it as necessary, valuable, and redeemable.

People who are good with their hands and mechanically inclined will walk around the tables filled of stuff and spot a broken item. They will pick it up, thoroughly analyze it, and decide to buy it. Why? They know how to fix it. And when they get the broken item to their workshop, they take it apart; each piece is inspected and vigorously cleaned. The broken parts are repaired and then the new owner carefully reassembles every component with the skill of a world-class surgeon. And the very item that others thought had little to no value now works better than ever.

Broken Is Not Bad

Did you know God scans the earth looking for broken things? In fact, God doesn't use it until it is broken. For example, when about 15,000 people were hungry and without food, Jesus took a little boy's lunch and broke the bread and fed the multitude.

I know it sounds weird, but broken things in God's hands last longer, and affect more people.

In Luke 7 Jesus illustrates the value of brokenness. The woman entered Simon the leper's house and made her way directly toward Jesus. Then she broke an alabaster box and poured the expensive perfume on Jesus' head. The perfume was a year's worth of wages. As long as it was in a container, it made no impact—its fragrance was concealed, benefiting no one. However, the moment the box was broken, Jesus received a blessing as it truly revealed how much she loved Him.

Peter, warming himself around a community campfire, was confronted about his relationship with Jesus. He denied ever knowing Jesus; and the Bible says after his denial Peter went out and wept bitterly. He was humiliated because hours earlier he boasted about how he would never deny Jesus. However after

Jesus' resurrection, Peter meet Him again on the shores of the Sea of Galilee and everything changed. Peter was a broken man, but he came back stronger than ever (Luke 22:54-62; Matthew 16:18).

When Christ was sharing the Lord's supper with His disciples, He held the bread and broke it and said, *"This is My body which is broken for you"* (1 Corinthians 11:24). Life came to us all because Jesus was broken.

Saul of Tarsus was a very proud man, highly educated, respectful reputation among the religious elite—and a persecutor of Christians. He looked at himself as being invincible and unbreakable. However, God had a different thought. On the road to Damascus (Acts 9) Jesus met Saul and in an instant everything shifted. He was powerless, blind, and utterly humiliated in front of those who traveled with him. In a moment he was broken. He humbled himself before the Lord; and the result, Saul became Paul—an apostle, church planter, and author of two-thirds of the New Testament.

In the Church's illustrious past, every great move of God the world has ever experienced came as a result of someone who was completely broken before the Lord. History reveals the more broken you are, the more usable you are to God. And to complicate the process, no one likes to be broken—our flesh fights it as much as possible.

Let me encourage you—don't discard your current situation of difficulty, it just may be God. Naturally, we do our best to preserve our dignity and life as we know it. I did. But God does His best to strip us so we come to the end ourselves. I love what Vance

Havner said, "God uses broken things. It takes broken soil to produce a crop, broken clouds to give rain, broken grain to give bread."

Jeremiah the prophet said, *"Break up your fallow ground, and do
not sow among thorns"* (Jeremiah 4:3). He knew that in order for
the earth to yield a healthy harvest, the ground had to be plowed
and the hard compacted dirt had to be broken up. May God come
to us and plow our hearts and break up the hard places. It will not
be pleasant, but it will be worth it.

> For whoever wants to save their life will lose it, but who-
> ever loses their life for me will find it (Matthew 16:25
> NIV).

I know I have said this before but I must say it again—all
the men and women whom God has mightily used were broken
and shattered.

One particular example is Jacob who was known for being a
deceiver, manipulator, liar, and trickster. He succeeded in deceiv-
ing his brother and father in order to steal the family blessing that
is designated for the firstborn. Over time, Jacob saw himself as he
really was, a deceiver. In his quest to be at peace with God, God
met him. Genesis 32:24 says Jacob wrestled with God all night. It
was here where God broke him and pierced him deeply.

His encounter with God took place in isolation, but manifested publicly—it always does. The Scriptures say from that day
forward, Jacob walked with a limp. You cannot wrestle with God
and remain the same.

Let the following passages encourage and prepare your heart
for more:

Psalm 51:17: *"The sacrifices of God are a broken spirit; a broken and a contrite heart—these, O God, You will not despise."*

Isaiah 57:15 (NIV): *"For this is what the high and exalted One says—he who lives forever, whose name is holy: 'I live in a high and holy place, but also with the one who is contrite and lowly in spirit, to revive the spirit of the lowly and to revive the heart of the contrite.'"*

Isaiah 66:2: *"'For all those things My hand has made, and all those things exist,' says the Lord. 'But on this one will I look: on him who is poor and of a contrite spirit, and who trembles at My word.'"*

We have to be willing to allow Him to break us. You cannot carry His glory without being broken. There will be no renewal, no revival, no awakening, and no glory until we come to the complete end of ourselves.

ENDNOTE

1. Nelson James, "All About Yard Sales"; https://www.signs.com/blog/all-about-yard-sales-info-graphic; accessed May 19, 2020.

23

ANGUISH

"All the true revivals have been born in prayer. When God's people become so concerned about the state of religion that they lie on their faces day and night in earnest supplication, the blessing will be sure to fall."
—E.M. BOUNDS

Charles Finney gave a dramatic explanation of what happened at one of his meetings when the glory and presence of God showed up:

> I had not spoken to them in this strain of direction, I should think more than a quarter of an hour, when all at once an awful solemnity seemed to settle down upon them; and something flashed over the congregation—a

kind of shimmering—as if there was some agitation in the atmosphere itself.

Finney added:

> The congregation began to fall from their seats; and they fell in every direction and cried for mercy. If I had had a sword in each hand I could not have cut them off their seats as fast as they fell. Indeed, nearly the whole congregation were either on their knees or prostrate, I should think, in less than two minutes from this first shock that fell upon them.

He concludes, "Everyone prayed for himself who was able to speak at all. I, of course was obliged to stop preaching, for they no longer paid any attention."[1]

In one of his soul-riveting sermons the late David Wilkerson, who stirred our nation to seek God, revealed a key ingredient for those who want to walk in the glory of God. He said,

> Whatever happened to anguish in the house of God? Whatever happened to anguish in the ministry? It is a word you don't hear in this pampered age. Anguish means extreme pain and distress. The emotions so stirred that it becomes painful, acute deeply felt inner pain because of conditions about you, in you, or around you. Anguish. Deep pain. Sorrow. Agony of God's heart.

He adds,

> All true passion is born out of anguish. All true passion for Christ comes out of a baptism of anguish. You search

the scriptures and you will find that when God determined to recover a ruined situation He would seek out a praying man and He would literally baptize Him in anguish.[2]

To have revival and the glory of God residing on us and our churches will take more than reverently sitting in church listening to motivational talks and sermons. It will take more than attending conferences and walking through prayer tunnels and having someone lay hands on us. There is more to it than that, much more.

James 4:9 is an unfamiliar passage for most and its application will not be congruent with the spirit of our culture. In fact, it is countercultural to the current flow of mainstream Christianity:

> *Lament and mourn and weep! Let your laughter be turned to mourning and your joy to gloom* (James 4:9).

I am convinced that understanding and applying this text in our lives is paramount to position ourselves and our churches to host His glory. Sadly, honestly, we have loss the value of lamenting and actually try to avoid it at all costs. When was the last time you heard your pastor address "lamenting" from the pulpit?

I assure you that not many sermons or small group studies have been developed on this passage; however, this expression is so vitally important to God that He named an entire book of the Bible, Lamentations.

What does it mean for a Christian to lament?

When we lament, we are releasing a passionate, deep-rooted expression of grief or sorrow because something is gruesomely wrong. In essence, when we lament we are so grieved that raw emotions come forth that are so intense that oftentimes it cannot be articulated with words.

Why would God instruct us to lament? What is the context of James 4? God is addressing His children to stop their sinful activities and to live their lives fully devoted to Jesus. God was saying, "turn to Me while you lament."

Can you imagine if believers worldwide fell under conviction and began to lament before the Lord for their carnality and subtle compromises? Oh what a difference it would make in every nation.

James included mourning as an acceptable response to the current conditions of the heart. To mourn means that we express sadness or sorrow, agonize, and are grieved about the condition of our hearts.

This is exactly what Isaiah did when he saw the Lord high and lifted up in perfect holiness upon His throne (Isaiah 6:1-6). The first word out of Isaiah's mouth is "Woe," which literally means great sorrow or distress. After observing God's holiness, Isaiah's hidden imperfections surfaced before his eyes and it caused him to repent with heartfelt sorrow (Isaiah 6:5).

Tragically, the "woe" is missing from our gatherings; it has been replaced by the "wow" factor in our church services. Leadership teams work hard on wowing and impressing their attenders and for the most part they are. Worshippers are wowed by the messages, the lights, the haze, the production, the environment—but I believe God wants the "woe" back in our meetings. This can take place when we are confronted with His holiness.

Then James added, weeping. Shedding of tears.

In my opinion due to an unbalanced interpretation of the grace of God and the constant emphasis that God approves of us regardless of how we live, the message of lamenting, mourning, and weeping are outside the cultural norm and mainstream Christianity. Again, when was the last time you heard from the pulpit the need for us to lament, mourn, and weep over our sins? This topic is virtually nonexistent.

Leonard Ravenhill said, "Our eyes are dry because our hearts are dry."[3] Revivalist Charles Finney correctly said, "There can be no revival when Mr. Amen and Mr. Wet-Eyes are not found in the audience."

The Church for the most part has forgotten how to weep before God over our sins. They feel no need to do so. Why? One of the reasons, as mentioned, is an improper understanding of the purpose of God's grace. Sadly, and I might add unintentionally, we have disgraced the grace of God by not emphasizing that grace was granted to pull you out of your condition—not to give you a free pass to remain there. The net result is that many have abused, manipulated, and applied grace to justify their sinful indulgences. People feel that God is indifferent about our actions. Nothing could be further from the truth.

Now, hearts have grown so cold in the Church that people are classified as undignified if they do show brokenness and emotion in the house of God. May we cry like Isaiah when he beheld the Lord in all of His glory, *"Woe is me for I am undone! Because I am a man of unclean lips, and I dwell in the midst of a people of unclean lips…"* (Isaiah 6:5).

You may think these emotions are excessive and unnecessary. Also, you may ask what are they grieving and lamenting over? James identifies the basis for the lamenting in the prior verse, *"Cleanse your hands, you sinners; and purify your hearts, you double-minded"* (James 4:8). James said, we need to lament because our lifestyle is foreign to the life God expects us to live. Our behavior doesn't match our confession as being saved and children of God.

I hear people all the time tell pastors and teachers, "Keep it positive, life is difficult enough. People don't want to go to church and have to deal with things that make them feel bad." Again, it is this mindset that has caused us to forget that our sins are grievous before God, the God who expects and commands His children to live holy lives.

People may argue that teaching and preaching about holy living in this culture is extreme and unnecessary, but I beg to differ. Here is an example of how far we have drifted away from holy, biblical expression.

On any given Friday or Saturday night, Christians who are genuinely saved, church-attending people who have been redeemed by the blood of Jesus will excitedly walk into a movie theatre to be entertained. The desire for entertainment or the movie theatre are not the issues. What they find entertaining is the issue and causes concern. They will purchase a ticket and wait in line to get their popcorn and drink before taking their seat. All of which will be enjoyed during the movie.

The movie they choose to watch at some point will use an array of crude language and may even show sexually explicit content.

And the most disheartening is that the actors will use the Lord's name in vain not just once, but multiple times throughout.

Yet there we are, sitting, watching, fully engaged, laughing, and being entertained by the very things that nailed Jesus to the cross. The very sins of darkness that He delivered us from we are now attracted to and amused by. How can this be? The expectation of what Christians do and how they should live has been so watered down that most people see nothing wrong with it and feel no conviction.

Take a step back for a moment and think how out of balance this is with what the Bible says, and how seared our consciences have become. Many Christians "believe" it is not a big deal; in fact, see no problem with it at all. However, it is not our belief system that dictates whether or not something is acceptable to the Lord. It is His standard alone—His Word, the Bible. Our definition of what is good and acceptable oftentimes does not equal what He classifies as good and acceptable.

Here's a thought. Can you imagine the apostle Paul in such a place? Perhaps taking his prodigy Timothy to go watch a movie with nude scenes and where the actors use the Lord's name in vain? Paul did address what his response would be when he wrote about such issues to the church at Ephesus:

> *Therefore be imitators of God as dear children. And walk in love, as Christ also has loved us and given Himself for us, an offering and a sacrifice to God for a sweet-smelling aroma. But fornication and all uncleanness or covetousness, **let it not even be named among you, as is fitting for saints**; neither filthiness, nor*

*foolish talking, nor coarse jesting, **which are not fitting**, but rather giving of thanks. For this you know, that no fornicator, unclean person, nor covetous man, who is an idolater, has any inheritance in the kingdom of Christ and God. Let no one deceive you with empty words, for because of these things the wrath of God comes upon the sons of disobedience. **Therefore do not be partakers with them. For you were once darkness, but now you are light in the Lord. Walk as children of light** (for the fruit of the Spirit is in all goodness, righteousness, and truth), finding out what is acceptable to the Lord. And **have no fellowship with the unfruitful works of darkness**, but rather expose them* (Ephesians 5:1-11).

Dreadfully, somewhere along our journey we have failed to remember the lacerated body of our Lord Jesus as His hands were tied above His head to a scourging post. His body was ruthlessly cut to shreds as they abused Him with a Roman whip. Oh how we have forgotten the image of a bloodied Jesus on the cross. While we sit in a theatre may we recall that His hands, feet, and side were pierced to set us free from the bondage of sin. May our eyes gaze into His eyes as blood and sweat pour from His brow and drip from His chin. While we eat the last of our candies, may we realize it was this, this behavior on the big screen that we now "enjoy," it was this that nailed Him to the cross.

The reason I am drawing attention to this is to shine a bright light on how far we have drifted away from biblical Christianity demonstrated by our separation from the world.

Some would say that what I am suggesting is legalism. Or that I am condemning people who exercise their liberty in Christ to live as they wish. My fervency on this issue is not driven by legalism, nor am I condemning anyone. I am making a point that the Church, in general, sees nothing wrong with being aligned with gross darkness—but God does.

The reason we should avoid the movies that are filled with godlessness is not because someone tells you that you should, but because you have such a love relationship with your Savior that you don't want to do anything that would grieve Him.

Ephesians 4:30 says, *"And do not grieve the Holy Spirit of God, by whom you were sealed for the day of redemption."* The word *grieve* means to cause to be sorrowful, to affect with sadness, cause grief, or to offend.

I am troubled that many in the Church just don't believe our choices, behaviors, and actions can offend God and grieve Jesus deeply. Some try to justify their behavior by saying, "It doesn't affect me, I can handle it." Oh, my friend, it does affect you—it stains your spirit and weakens your anointing. You are yielding areas of your life to the devil by opening the eye and ear gates into your soul. The Bible cautions us to not give the devil any opportunity to take advantage of us.

Ephesians 4:27 (NIV) says, *"Do not give the devil a foothold."* Plus, Peter counseled his fellow believers with these words, *"Beloved, I beg you as sojourners and pilgrims, abstain from fleshly lusts which war against the soul"* (1 Peter 2:11). Paul became even more pointed in his conviction when it came to our relationship with the Holy Spirit and sin in First Thessalonians 5:19, *"Do not quench the Spirit."* His warning—do not behave in such a way that extinguishes the fire of God. Then Paul adds this little nugget, *"Abstain from every form of evil"* (1 Thessalonians 5:22).

It is curious how we were convicted and felt awful because of our sin prior to coming to Christ— but then justify it in our lives afterward. This ought *not* be our disposition. There should be a greater awareness of what offends the Lord and a resolute commitment to do whatever it takes to abstain from such things. Why? Because you love Him.

I know this a hard truth to read, but it is necessary. Again, it isn't about the movies—it's about being aware of our choices and behaviors that can grieve and quench the Spirit of God, whom we so desperately need.

My wife and I have been married for more than thirty-five years. I love her deeply and I would never think of doing anything to cause her to be grieved, pained, sorrowful, or doubt my love for her. I don't make that decision based on legalism nor am I guilted into doing right, no. My relationship with her matters. Her feelings matter.

Jesus deserves the same devotion and respect from each of us. He is a jealous God, He loves us, and He wants us to love Him back. Not just with words but with how we live.

Archbishop Fulton Sheen said, "The more intense the love, the less we think of a sacrifice involved to secure what we love."

How long has it been since you have wept over the condition of your heart? Ask the Lord now to allow you to see your heart as it truly is.

ENDNOTES

1. Lex Loizides, "Demonstrations of the Spirit's Power—Charles Finney"; Church History Review, June 28, 2012; https://lexloiz .wordpress.com/2012/06/18/demonstrations-of-the-spirits -power-charles-finney/; accessed June 2, 2020.
2. David Wilkerson, "A Call to Anguish"; August 5, 2012; https:// www.youtube.com/watch?v=NPPmpGFF5jE; accessed June 2, 2020.
3. Leonard Ravenhill, *Why Revival Tarries* (Grand Rapids, MI: Baker Publishing Co., 1987), 51.

Part Five

PRAYER POWER

24

WHAT DO
SATANISTS FEAR?

*"There has never been a spiritual awakening in any
country or locality that did not begin in united prayer."*

—A.T. PIERSON

Samuel Chadwick said, "The one concern of the devil is to keep Christians from praying. He fears nothing from prayerless studies, prayerless work, and prayerless religion. He laughs at our toil, mocks at our wisdom, but trembles when we pray." The imagery is fascinating.

The Merriam-Webster dictionary defines *tremble* as "to shake involuntarily; to be affected with great fear or anxiety." I believe Chadwick is correct. The devil shakes and trembles at our praying.

Imagine it. Every time we go to the Lord in prayer, the devil gets extremely nervous and stressed to the point of trembling! No wonder he tries to disrupt our prayer life. He fears an effective, praying person more than anything on earth.

I recall a testimony of a leading pastor who told an interesting story about the power of prayer. Years ago a youth pastor at a large church along with his ministerial team had been witnessing to a satanist and eventually led him to the Lord. The life change was dramatic and after a while the youth pastor sat down and asked the former satanist a few questions. One of which was, "As a Satanist, what did you fear the most about Christians?"

His reply was quick and to the point. "We have seen what is accomplished when they pray. The response in the spiritual is very significant when a believer prays in the Spirit. We (as satanists) tried our best to prevent and discourage it at all costs."

Why do satanists fear when God's people pray in tongues? For starters, the believer is praying for the perfect will of God to be accomplished and evil despises the harm that comes to their kingdom as a result.

Interestingly, another satanist revealed something similar, "We fear churches and Christians who pray in tongues." He added, "We are able to see in the spirit realm and we know when they (Christians) pray in tongues because we see an increase in angelic activity as angels dart across the sky sent on divine assignments."

Bless the Lord, you His angels, who excel in strength, who do His word, heeding the voice of His word (Psalm 103:20).

Let this encourage you. This should motivate you to intercede and pray with greater focus and tenacity. Think about the magnitude prayer has on God's Kingdom as angels are commissioned to go on your behalf when you pray. Could this be one of the reasons the apostle Paul encouraged us to labor in prayer and to pray without ceasing? (See Colossians 4:12 and 1 Thessalonians 5:17.)

Let us be ever mindful that prayer is spiritual warfare at the highest level. The enemy will fight you at every turn and try to impede the angels moving on your behalf in response to your prayers.

It happened in Daniel 10:12-13:

> *Then he said to me, "Do not fear, Daniel, for from the first day that you set your heart to understand, and to humble yourself before your God, your words were heard; and I have come because of your words. But the prince of the kingdom of Persia withstood me twenty-one days; and behold, Michael, one of the chief princes, came to help me, for I had been left alone there with the kings of Persia."*

This is why we pray all the more; we don't stop. We persevere and pray until we get a breakthrough, until we get the full assurance of God's purpose being accomplished. Every time we pray believing prayers that are God's will, we know God hears us. First John 5:14-15 tells us:

> *Now this is the confidence that we have in Him, that if we ask anything according to His will, **He hears us**. And*

if we know that He hears us, whatever we ask, we know
that we have the petitions that we have asked of Him.

I love the Amplified Version of James 5:16: "...*The heartfelt and persistent prayer of a righteous man (believer) can accomplish much [when put into action and made effective by God—it is dynamic and can have tremendous power].*"

As a result, much is accomplished for the Kingdom. This verse reveals that our prayers, when God gets involved, are dynamic and will release tremendous power.

25

MAKING THE DEPOSIT

*"True revival cannot be worked up; it
can only be prayed down!"*
—EDDIE HYATT

Reverend William Reid speaking to his fellow brothers
had this to say about prayer:

Why is there so little anxiety to get time to pray? Why is
there so little forethought in the laying out of time and
employment, so as to secure a large portion of each day
for prayer? Why is there so much speaking yet so little
prayer? Why is there so much running to and fro, yet so
little prayer? Why so much bustle and business, yet so little prayer? Why so many meetings with our fellow men,

yet so few meetings with God? Why so little begin alone, so little thirsting of the soul for the calm, sweet hours of unbroken solitude when God and his child hold fellowship together as if they could never part? It is this want that not only injures our own growth in grace but makes us such unprofitable servants of Christ.[1]

A few months after the North Georgia Revival began, God's amazing glory was increasing exponentially and we were witnessing remarkable miracles take place at our altars and in the baptismal waters. The crowds were increasing as well as the needs of those in attendance. The pressure on me and the church was great and increasing daily.

Out of desperation I made a phone call and spoke to Pastor John Kilpatrick, who pastored Brownsville Assembly of God during the Pensacola, Florida, Outpouring. I asked him how we could sustain revival and the presence of God in our services, plus meet the needs that were walking through our doors.

He didn't hesitate. He said, "Todd, the key is to pray. You and your people must pray." Then he added, "Prayer needs to be seen as a deposit. A deposit in the Spirit that the minister or ministry can withdraw from the very next service."

I never looked at prayer as a deposit. It makes perfect sense in the natural and the spiritual.

For example, when you don't make the necessary financial deposit in the natural and you go to the bank to withdraw some money, you can't. Why? Nothing has been deposited, there is nothing there. In order to withdraw, you have to make a deposit.

Here is another example. What happens when you write a check or use your debit card to purchase something, but there are insufficient funds in your account? The bank may cover your lack of funds once or twice, but they won't continue to do so; in most cases they will fine you because of the overdraft. This means you try to purchase something with funds you have not deposited.

This happens in the Spirit during church services all the time. Broken and shattered lives walk into our sanctuaries needing an encounter with God. Their lives are in ruins, their bodies are sick, their homes are shattered, and their addictions are gruesome. Sadly, far too many at the end of our church services walk out without encountering God's power; we were not able to help them. They came to receive, but we had nothing to give them; we asked God to touch them, but they left the same. Why? Not enough prayer deposit was made during the week. Of course we give them steps, formulas, and principles to follow—but no power and glory to encounter.

In some restaurants, managers display their food items behind a glass or on a table, and place a sign that reads, "Display Only." It looks real, however, it is a mock-up of the real thing. It is waxed food, painted and made to look like the real meal. Far too many of our church experiences are similar. People come hungry, hurting, and needing an encounter with God, but there is little to no glory in our buildings; therefore, we are guilty of "displaying" what God could do and that is it. In the body of Christ we have to get beyond the "Display Only" environment and create the culture that hosts God's glory so people can come and experience His power.

What is the issue and why is this occurring? Is the preaching from our modern pulpits the problem? Is the contemporary worship scene the issue? To these questions I answer, "No." People leave our church meetings not encountering the Spirit and glory of God because the ministers, leaders, and congregations are failing to make the necessary deposit in prayer. The little emphasis and engagement with prayer has left us with an insufficient amount of power to meet the needs of a broken world. People are coming to the house of bread, and we have at best only crumbs to give them.

Reap What You Sow

Paul says that we reap what we sow (Galatians 6:7). This includes our prayer life. He says in Second Corinthians 9:6, *"He who sows sparingly will also reap sparingly, and he who sows bountifully will also reap bountifully."*

The level of glory and power in our lives and ministries is directly proportionate to the deposit we make in prayer: *"...but he who sows to the Spirit will of the Spirit reap everlasting life. And let us not grow weary while doing good, for in due season we will reap if we do not lose heart"* (Galatians 6:8-9).

Pastor Kilpatrick's instruction to me had a profound impact. We now see prayer as a deposit. Our church makes five significant prayer deposits each week; and on Sundays during our services, we withdraw from that account. Since we have "prayed the price" God shows up and does what He did in the book of Acts.

Dr. J.B. Phillips, who gave us the Phillips New Testament, says of the first chapters of Acts:

This is the church of Jesus Christ before it became fat and out of breath by prosperity. This is the church of Jesus Christ before it became muscle bound by over organization. This is the church of Jesus Christ where they didn't gather together a group of intellectuals to study psychosomatic medicine, they just healed the sick. This is the church of Jesus Christ where they did not say prayers, but they prayed in the Holy Ghost."[2]

Early in the revival our church grasped this truth.

Stage 4 Breast Cancer

It was the worst day of her life. A few days earlier she felt an unusual high level of pain in her body and decided a trip to the doctor was warranted. The news Loraine Barge received was devastating, "Stage 4 Metazoic Breast Cancer." The PET scan shockingly revealed over fifty aggressive cancerous lesions throughout her body. This diagnosis was a death sentence.

After consulting with the oncologist, she, along with her husband John, agreed to attack the cancer through a less invasive approach, oral chemo. They decided to fight on both a physical and spiritual level.

The Lord specifically instructed her to take communion every day to remind her of what He did on the cross, and also to read out loud the healing Scriptures in her Bible.

The doctors told her that the treatment path she chose, oral chemo, probably would not cure her but has the potential to slow down the spread of the cancer and perhaps, at best, contain it. They did not say or even imply that the oral chemo would exterminate the cancer. The projections and prognosis were disheartening to say the least.

At the time, Loraine and her husband, John, lived in Brunswick, Georgia, which is five and half hours away from Dawsonville. A friend of hers who was aware of the revival shared a video of one of our powerful baptismal services. Not long afterward, another friend actually attended the North Georgia Revival and was healed of high blood pressure. This increased Loraine's desire to attend the revival in North Georgia.

The more she heard, the greater her faith became. She told John she wanted to travel to Dawsonville to encounter Jesus in the fire water.

On October 28, a Sunday afternoon, they arrived early for church and sat in the sanctuary to enjoy the sweet presence of God. The Lord's manifest presence was already in the building and increased throughout the night. After the minister preached, the call was given for all who wanted to encounter the Lord in the water to come forward. Loraine and John anxiously walked up the five altar stairs and onto the platform. They cordially took their place in line patiently waiting for their time to be baptized. They closely watched as dozens of people were consumed with God's fire in the water.

Four hours later it was her turn. John and Loraine descended the steps into the baptismal pool and with each step she encountered more of His presence, more of His glory. God was meeting them in the water.

As they stepped onto the bottom step, she made the turn and slowly made her way to the front of the baptismal tank where Pastor Marty was waiting. He greeted them with such tenderness and compassion, but I could see the concern on her face.

About the experience, she said these exact words:

> When we entered the water, Pastor Marty asked us the usual, "What is your name, where are you from, and what are you in the water for?" I said I was diagnosed with stage 4 cancer and it would be really cool if after my baptism all the lesions were gone.
>
> Pastor Marty stopped and asked everyone to pray for us and then he baptized us.
>
> When I went down in the water, I felt like I was in a cocoon and I heard a song being sung over me in the spirit. The song was "Can I have this Dance" by Anne Murray. This was a life-changing experience, just floating in the water, having Jesus sing a love song over me.
>
> After a while (I'm not sure how long) I came to, and realized there were 100 or more people waiting to be baptized and I was thinking I better get up so they could have a turn. Just then, the young woman who was supporting my body, told me not to rush and just let the Lord do what He wanted to do.

One of the symptoms of her aggressive cancer was she had difficulty moving her neck from side to side. Her neck was constantly stiff and extremely sore.

Loraine continues:

After I got out of the water I quickly noticed I could turn my head without pain.

The next day after the baptism I had a scheduled PET scan. The results would take several days to receive. On Tuesday after my baptism at Christ Fellowship Church, a friend and I went for a walk.

The week before my baptism I was only able to walk about three houses down from my house, as I would get lightheaded and have much pain. This particular day, two days after baptism, my friend and I walked two miles! I was not sure if it was a fluke, so I tried it again the next day and was still able to walk two miles!

The day after I walked two miles, I returned to the doctor to review the PET scan results. NO CANCEROUS LESIONS FOUND IN MY BODY!!!

Over 50 cancerous lesions gone! Up to this point, for three months I had been taking an oral chemo pill that is designed to help slow the growth of the cancer, but Jesus did exceedingly abundantly above all that I could ask or think!

The PA that was treating me had tears in her eyes as she reviewed the scan, and she said this was the third miracle she has seen in 20 years. The doctor said my results were not typical. My Jesus is not typical!!! His love for us is overwhelming. He desires to see us healed and walk in wholeness.

It was a night that would change not only her life but the lives of thousands of people all around the world. Her story went viral and to this day many people have found complete healing in the waters as a result of her testimony.

Thankfully, our church made the necessary prayer deposit in order to be used of God to meet her enormous need. May we no longer be "Display Only" churches.

ENDNOTES

1. Henry Fish, *Handbook of Revivals* (Hess Publications, 1998), Chapter 19: "Are You Revived?"
2. Leonard Ravenhill sermon, "Weeping Between the Porch and the Altar."

26

EXTRAORDINARY PRAYER

*"If your church says they want revival, check out their
midweek prayer service. Someone may be lying."*
—Joe Joe Dawson

One of the greatest struggles believers face is the discipline of prayer. Often our schedules are so full that we are either too busy to pray or too exhausted.

The devil knows it is in the arena of prayer where victories are won or lost and will use any means at his disposal to keep us from it.

Richard Sibbes, an Anglican theologian in the 16th century, made an acute observation about prayer, "When we go to God by prayer, the devil knows we go to fetch strength against him, and therefore he opposes us all he can."

These are exceptional days we are living in and a nonchalant approach to prayer can no longer be our disposition. We must recognize the devil's intent to distract us from prayer and commit to do whatever is necessary to have victory in this area.

We would be wise not to ignore what Jonathan Edwards said about prayer, "...to promote explicit agreement and visible union of God's people in *extraordinary prayer*." Edward's last two words are interesting—"extraordinary prayer." This implies there must be ordinary prayer, routine, typical prayer.

So, what does extraordinary prayer look like? It is a type of prayer that is more than a passing thought or practice. Extraordinary prayer is when your prayer life and faith cost you something. Perhaps, it is when you pray all night, you are overcome with deep sorrow, or joy, even a deep groaning and/or intercessions may come upon you. In my opinion, it is this type of extraordinary prayer that is essential for us to have a move of God.

Matthew Henry, a biblical scholar, wrote, "When God intends great mercy for His people, the first thing He does is to set them a-praying."[1]

During the sixteenth-century Scottish Reformation there was an individual who believed that just one man is a majority with God. He prayed for his country to be saved and dedicated his life to that end. It is said that Mary Queen of Scots had a greater dread of the prayers of John Knox than of all the armies of Europe.

Oh may the wicked principalities of the earth fear the praying Church. May presidents, prime ministers, and third-world dictators fear the man or woman who has the attention of God and who prays extraordinary prayers.

These are unordinary times that require an unordinary response. The evidence proves that evil is spreading and is invading all aspects of our society, it is affecting every facet of life. Who will resist it? Who will raise the wall of opposition in the spirit? Who will meet with the Lord and on their knees push back the darkness? Who, if and when necessary, will wrestle with principalities and powers until the light arises in the darkness? Who will pray extraordinary prayers?

Even in the darkness light dawns for the upright...
(Psalm 112:4 NIV).

Not long ago on Facebook I posted a quote that caught people off guard, and I might add it received a tremendous amount of responses. Here it is: "Before we launch a campaign to get prayer reinstated into the public schools, let's do a campaign that gets prayer back into our churches."

When will the Church gather again, not simply to worship or hear another sermon, but to pray? I mean pray—to cry out for His face, His intervention, and His glory.

I am encouraged because more and more pastors are seeing this as the greatest need of the Church. In fact, as I look out over the horizon I see a vast army of individuals who will begin to meet in small gatherings to pray for the glory of God to manifest in their churches. Ordinary people who are not specifically gifted with intercession, but who long and desire to see the Kingdom of God manifest upon the church they attend. The move of God in Dawsonville, Georgia, was and is a direct result of such people—and if it can happen with us, it can happen anywhere.

In his book *In the Day of Thy Power,* Arthur Wallis wrote, "From the day of Pentecost, there has not been one great spiritual awakening in any land which has not begun in a union of prayer, though only among two or three; and no such outward, upward movement has continued after such prayer meetings have declined."[2]

Charles Spurgeon, the "Prince of Preachers" wrote, "The prayer meeting is the place to meet with the Holy Ghost, and this is the way to get His mighty power! If we would have Him, we must meet in greater numbers; we must pray with greater fervency, we must watch with greater earnestness, and believe with firmer steadfastness. The prayer meeting…is the appointed place for the reception of power."[3]

Who among us will go without food until the glory of God comes? Who will stand and remain in the prayer chamber until the tangible presence of God invades our churches, our schools, and cities? The eyes of God are scanning our churches and neighborhoods looking for the ones who will pray till Heaven comes. Who will pray extraordinary prayers?

The disciples asked the Lord, "Jesus, teach us to pray." Notice, they didn't cry out to learn how to raise the dead, cast out devils, or heal the sick. They didn't even ask Him how to be a better teacher or communicator. No, they knew the secret of Jesus' ministry—His prayer life.

The book of Acts and Paul's epistles reveal that the early Church followed Jesus' example. They knew prayer was not just *part* of their success—it was the *reason* for their effectiveness. For example, in Acts 4 the believers gathered to pray after Peter and John were released from prison. Here is what happened: *"And when they had prayed, the place where they were assembled together was shaken; and they were all filled with the Holy Spirit, and they spoke the word of God with boldness"* (Acts 4:31).

The early Church gave themselves to prayer.

Leonard Ravenhill, in his masterpiece of a book, *Why Revival Tarries*, wrote:

> Poverty-stricken as the Church is today in many things, she is most stricken here, in the place of prayer. We have many organizers, but few agonizers; many players and payers, few pray-ers; many singers, few clingers; lots of pastors, few wrestlers; many fears, few tears; much fashion, little passion; many interferers, few intercessors; many writers, but few fighters. Failing here, we fail everywhere.[4]

William Booth, had the task of inspiring and challenging a group of hard-preaching but ineffective evangelists. His message to them was simple, "Try tears, try tears."

What these men are saying falls under the category of "extraordinary prayers." Our approach to the world has to change. Our current strategies and approach to reach the world must stand behind the prayer movement of our ministries. A straightforward commitment to erect the private and public prayer chamber must begin now. There is no other way—a rebirth of the two is uncompromisable.

ENDNOTES

1. Arthur Wallis, *In the Day of Thy Power* (Ft. Washington, PA: CLC Publications, 2010), 112.
2. Ibid.
3. Bryan Galloway, "The Importance of Corporate Prayer According to Charles Spurgeon"; Pray for Revival!, January 21, 2014; https:// prayforrevival.wordpress.com/2014/01/21/the-importance-of -corporate-prayer-according-to-charles-spurgeon/; accessed June 2, 2020.
4. Leonard Ravenhill, *Why Revival Tarries*, 23.

27

WHERE ARE
THE JOABS?

*"Every great movement of God can be
traced to a kneeling figure."*
—Dwight L. Moody

Three thousand years ago David was made king of Israel and he quickly decided that Jerusalem, the Holy City, was to be the capital of Israel. Immediately he and all the Israelites marched to Jerusalem to overtake the crown jewel of the Middle East. However, there was a small problem—Jerusalem was a Canaanite city occupied by the Jebusites. This wasn't an ordinary city; it was so well built and fortified no nation had been able to conquer it. The towers were large and the walls impenetrable.

But David was determined to make Jerusalem the capital of his kingdom. He marched ahead with his army and when he arrived, he brazenly challenged the Jebusites. In return, the Jebusites mockingly said to him, *"You shall not come in here!"* (1 Chronicles 11:5). In other words, there's no way you're going to enter Jerusalem.

Then the Jebusites took the ridicule to the next level. They positioned lame and the blind people on top of the wall to defend against any hopeless attack. They said to David, *"the blind and the lame will repel you"* (2 Samuel 5:6).

When King David recognized that the city was unconquerable by traditional means, he devised an alternate plan. David, an expert military strategist, quickly identified their only weakness, their watering system.

Here is the epic moment. David gathers his troops to give a speech. It's an opportunity to boost the morale and call for great sacrifice. He stands and decrees, *"Whoever climbs up by way of the water shaft and defeats the Jebusites (the lame and the blind…), he shall be chief and captain"* (2 Samuel 5:8).

Joab Steps Up

David aggressively employs an uncommon strategy to defeat the enemy, and he is looking for one man to shift the odds in his favor. He waits. Then an unlikely individual comes forward, the king's nephew, Joab the son of Zeruiah. Joab's name means "Yahweh is father."

No one in the camp saw this coming, all were surprised. However, Joab's one step changed his life and the nation of Israel forever.

David commissions Joab, on what many thought was a suicide mission. He was sending his nephew on a covert operation to infiltrate the city via the waterway. Joab would climb, swim, and crawl his way through the water ducts and eventually emerge inside the fortress of Jerusalem. His family and friends say their goodbyes and wish him well, for they know they may never see him again.

While it is still dark, perhaps the wee hours of the morning, he departs. His aim is to penetrate the city while the occupants were in their homes fast asleep.

Joab maneuvers his way through the damp and musty waterway. He couldn't use a torch to light his way, he didn't want to attract any attention—he was in the pitch dark. He had to remain quiet, each step had to be carefully calculated and measured. Any unusual sound could cause an investigative response by the Jebusites. The way was slippery and dangerous.

After an intense journey he sees light flickering at the end of the tunnel. He approaches the opening with extreme caution. He is soaking wet and perhaps cold and exhausted. He sticks his head out of the opening like a prairie dog coming out of its hole concerned about approaching eagles looking for a nice meal. He looks to the left and the right to see if there are any soldiers on guard or citizens who could sound the alarm that there was an intruder. Miraculously, he found no one.

After Joab exits the tunnel, as quickly as possible he quietly makes his way to the city gates. No Jebusite notices him so he walks right to the armored gates and with great force pushes them open. On the other side, David's soldiers were waiting and ready to move forward. As soon as the gates cracked open they rushed through and mercilessly annihilated every inhabitant in the city.

We Must Step Up

I find it interesting the city was impenetrable, and on all accounts David's dream of conquering the city seemed hopeless. But one adventurous young man believed in the king's vision and volunteered to take up the challenge.

Without question the devil and his hordes have our society, community, and churches under siege. Darkness has overtaken our cities. The enemy takes advantage of every opportunity to mock God, His principles, as well as the people of God. And those same spirits of wickedness shout to us, "You cannot come in here!"

To some the enemy's voice is intimidating and many shrink in fear. Sadly, others look at the condition that our world is in and say there is no hope, no way we can change things.

I agree the challenge is daunting. The devil's strongholds and fortresses look overbearing, but God has a bodacious plan and He needs us to step forward and say, "Here I am. I am willing to pay the price and take the risk."

The good news is that it doesn't take a large number of people to crush the kingdom of darkness and its power over a city or church. But it does take someone. Someone has to step forward, one who is willing to leave the safety of the familiar and the comfortable. An individual who, if necessary, is prepared to walk alone through the damp cold tunnel to penetrate behind enemy lines.

For the eyes of the Lord run to and fro throughout the whole earth, to show Himself strong on behalf of those whose heart is loyal to Him. In this you have done foolishly; therefore from now on you shall have wars (2 Chronicle 16:9).

Can you imagine what might happen if one soul from every church wrestled with God until revival came? That would positively change the world as we know it.

Charles Finney the great revival preacher, had this to say about someone stepping forward and working to overthrow darkness:

Generally there are but few professors of religion that know anything about this spirit of prayer which prevails with God. I have been amazed to see such accounts as are often published about revivals, as if the revival had come without any cause—nobody knew why or wherefore. I have sometimes inquired into such cases, when it had been given out that nobody knew anything about it, until one Sabbath they saw in the face of the congregation that God was there; or they saw it in their conference room, or prayer meeting, and were astonished at the mysterious sovereignty of God in bringing in a revival without any apparent connection with means.

Now mark me! Go and inquire among the obscure members of the church, and you will always find that somebody had been praying for revival, and was expecting it—some man or woman had been agonizing in prayer for the salvation of sinners until the blessing was gained. This person perhaps woke everyone out of their sleep so that they jumped up, rubbed their eyes, and could not quite understand where the sudden excitement came from. Even if only so few know of the responsibility of a revival, you can be assured that someone held watch on the tower and did not cease with begging until the blessing was there.[1]

I understand in our culture of self-preservation, busyness, and easy believism that only a few are poised to step forward to pay the price in order to open the gates so the fire of God can invade the Church. Far too many are content and consequently unaware of the war in the spirit world. However, there are those among us who will rise to the occasion and traverse through danger to open the spiritual gates so God's glory can fall upon us once again.

Maybe someone would pray as did Isaiah:

> Oh, that you would rend the heavens and come down, that the mountains would tremble before you! As when fire sets twigs ablaze and causes water to boil, come down to make your name known to your enemies and cause the nations to quake before you! (Isaiah 64:1-2 NIV)

ENDNOTE

1. "No Revival Without the Spirit of Prayer," Christian Assemblies International; https://www.cai.org/bible-studies/no-revival -without-spirit-prayer; accessed May 20, 2020.

28

SPIRIT OF TRAVAIL

*"Everyone wants to walk in the power of Christ, but
who is willing to walk the prayer life of Christ?"*
—RICK PINNO

Being present in the hospital room with my wife as she gave birth to our boys was the most amazing experience of my life. Witnessing my sons take their first breath was truly remarkable.

However, while at the hospital, moments before my first son's birth, I made a huge mistake, one that nearly cost me my life. Let me explain.

Karen was dilated and her contractions were a few minutes apart. This was our first child and we were both excited. We thought her labor would be a few short hours and then she would give birth. Well, Ty had other plans. He wanted to stay inside the warm womb as long as he could. I had never seen Karen in such discomfort, the pain was indescribable.

When I thought things were calming down a little, I decided to step out for a few minutes as a friend brought me a hamburger and french fries from McDonald's. While I was out retrieving my meal, the birthing pains dramatically increased. Unbeknown to me, Karen evidently developed a heightened since of smell, which made me an unsuspecting innocent animal walking into a trap.

After consuming my burger outside the room, I gleefully walked back inside eating my bag of fries. I don't know what set her off exactly—the smile on my face, the happy walk, or the aroma of greasy french fries—but it did. I can now see how she had a problem with all three of my actions. She was trying to push out a 7-pound baby—and I'm stuffing my face with a burger and smelly, greasy fries. Not good. Honestly, I thought it was the end for me. The look she gave me needed no interpretation or explanation, it was brutal, otherworldly, not at all like my dear Karen. But all was forgiven…eventually.

On a more serious note, what amazed me the most was her commitment to give birth to our sons. She had the strength to keep pushing even when she was fatigued and experiencing an unbearable amount of trauma. She kept pushing when she didn't think she wasn't making much of a difference. She kept at it, she travailed greatly because she knew there was no other way—she had to give birth to our son.

It find it interesting and I think you will to that the Bible compares prayer with the travail of childbirth.

Birthing Position

A severe drought came to the land of Israel. Elijah witnessed the devastation it was having on the people of God. His response was to pray to seek God's help. As Elijah began to pray, the Bible says he crouched down with his head between his knees. This was the birthing position of that day. Obviously Elijah was not giving birth to a natural child, but was giving birth to God's plan for the earth. By his prayers and his relentless intercession, God sent the much-needed rain that ended a devastating drought.

Women will tell you the closer they are to giving birth the birthing pangs are the most intense. She knows she can't quit, she has to persevere; a child needs her to keep pushing. Often during the final stages of delivery a husband or coach is by her side encouraging her to, "Push and breathe, push and breathe, push and breathe." And at last the final big push is necessary for the delivery of the newborn child.

Prayer Is Hard and Difficult

Most would agree that prayer is the most difficult element and practice of our Christian walk. A commitment to pray is not easy— your flesh will fight it at every opportunity. In addition, it will be exhausting, messy, frustrating, and at times painful, because when you pray you are waring in the Spirit. You are battling for the advancement of the Kingdom of God in your life and the world; therefore, the enemy will oppose you at every opportunity.

Our greatest calling from God is to pray. Absolutely nothing moves God more than prayer. The million dollar question is this: Who will take the birthing position and not stop pushing until His glory descends?

Leonard Ravenhill, who had much to say about prayer, left us with this nugget, "At God's counter there are no sale days, for the price for revival is ever the same—travail."

> For as soon as Zion travailed, she brought forth her children (Isaiah 66:8 KJV).

My sincere prayer is that a travailing spirit will come upon the people of God. The spirit that calls us to push until revival is birthed in our own heart and then our church.

Who will pick up this mantle?

In the epic sermon, "The Story of God's Mighty Acts," Charles Spurgeon echoed a clarion call for all of God's children:

> Oh! Men and brethren, what would this heart feel if I could but believe that there were some among you who would go home and pray for a revival of religion— men whose faith is large enough, and their love fiery enough to lead them from this moment to exercise unceasing intercessions that God would appear among us and do wondrous thing here, as in the times of former generations.

One of my favorite historical revivals took place on the Hebrides Islands in Scotland in 1949. There were two wonderful Christian ladies, sisters Christine and Peggy Smith, one was 84 and the other 82. Peggy was blind and Christine was nearly doubled over due to the crippling effect of arthritis. They prayed night and day for revival. Before long their prayers stirred the hearts of a small group of men to pray in a barn three nights a week from 10 p.m. to 3 a.m.

Evangelist Duncan Campbell was soon invited to Lewis Island of the Hebrides. The host pastors asked him to speak to a gathering of 300 people in a church. The place was filled to capacity. This first service lasted for two hours—9 p.m. until 11 p.m.—and it was a glorious service.

Duncan Campbell didn't realize that outside the church were hundreds more people who had gathered to encounter God. They were desperate and their hearts ached with conviction of sin.

When he was told of those outside, he and the local pastors immediately started ministering to the enormous crowd outside the church. Then someone summoned Duncan Campbell to the side and told him he had to go to the police station.

"Why, what is wrong?" he asked. He was told there were 400 people there who were confessing their sins and faults and crying out for mercy—and the police didn't know what to do with them.

Campbell left the seeking and desperate souls at the church and traveled a mile on a dirt road to the police station. As he journeyed, he heard moaning and wailing from people from all walks of life who were lying in ditches, calling out to God for His mercy and grace. They were broken and crushed under the weight of God's convicting Spirit.

This sort of response was taking place throughout the lovely islands of Lewis and Harris. It was God's Spirit moving upon a people because two sisters grabbed hold of the heart of God and the world was dramatically touched.

There is no "man-made" shortcut to revival. Time on our knees releases the Spirit of God on our land and gives us the much-needed rain of His Spirit.

Throughout the centuries, history has taught us there has been one common denominator to genuine moves of God—prayer; earnest, desperate, fervent prayer was at the center of each awakening and revival. Talent doesn't attract God; however, a travailing intercessor does.

Charles Finney was a strategic figure in the Second Great Awakening and was quoted as saying, "Revival is no more a miracle than a crop of wheat. Revival comes from heaven when heroic souls enter the conflict determined to win or die—or if need be, to win and die."

Part Six

LIFE AND DEATH DECISIONS

29

IT'S MESSY

"When Holy God draws near in true revival, people come under terrible conviction of sin. The outstanding feature of spiritual awakening has been the profound consciousness of the presence and holiness of God."
—HENRY BLACKABY

Over the years, at times, God has moved mightily among His people with incredible visitations of His power. Many have witnessed "revival" come to a church and then within a matter of weeks the revival seemed to be over. What started as an undeniable encounter with God quickly became a memory. Why? What went wrong?

One thing I have discovered is that the glory of God is heavy, very heavy. When God settles down on a church, He sets His glory on the shoulders of the men and women of that local congregation; they carry it, manage it, maneuver it, host it, and pastor it.

Sadly, not every church can adequately host and carry His glory. There are multiple reasons for why they can't or choose not to—perhaps they don't have the desire, infrastructure, focus, fortitude, temperament, prayer emphasis, determination, culture, or discipline. Let me explain.

Everybody wants revival, right?

In the early days of revival everyone is thrilled at the heavenly invasion and ecstatic to be part of a genuine move of the Spirit. Their lives as well as their family and friends are heavily impacted. They are eyewitness to Kingdom conflicts and physical expressions of the glory of God that leave most awestruck.

At first, the revival is exhilarating, engaging, and most everyone is filled with wonderment at all that God is doing. However, it doesn't take very long for people to discover revival has another side to it. A painful side. Living under and in the glory of God, as magnificent as that is, demands more from the local congregation and its leaders than some are willing to give.

For example, you can't host God's glory and maintain revival and continue to accommodate sinful habits and compromises. When revival first comes, God is gracious and allows us time to manage our personal walk with Him as He highlights the insufficiencies in our relationship with Him. We normally are okay with this because it is obvious that those issues need to be dealt with, they are the surface issues of our life.

However, the attitude toward God and the revival shifts when He begins to shed His convicting light of purity on the hidden dark rooms of the heart. You know, the places and things that are entrenched and are seen by us as "no big deal." When God goes to these places, it is usually at this point when things get a little more difficult, in fact problematic.

As the glory of God increases, the call for us to walk circumspectly also increases. He demands more from us—personal holiness, for example. This is where many begin to find fault with a move of God, pull away from it, or criticize those leading it. Why? Many people don't want to deal with those tucked-away issues; therefore, it is easier to blame others for not participating than admit to having things they are not ready to surrender to the Lord.

I remember when the glory of God hit our church. The congregation was amazed and delighted that the Kingdom of God was manifesting in our church. As the weeks went on into months, the Lord's conviction increased and so did His demand for righteousness. I started noticing more and more people were no longer supporting or participating in the revival. This greatly troubled me; so much so that I made a comment from the pulpit, "Hey, God is here. He is changing us and we are seeing people healed and lives forever changed. Why aren't you part of this move of God?" It wasn't long before I received the following message from someone who attended our church:

> Some of us come to church and have been on the "outside" of this revival, just to watch, but it is not possible. This is not a spectator sport. If you are in the house, God is working on you. He is opening up my eyes to things

I don't want to deal with and didn't know I needed to deal with…it's been simpler to be a zombie until revival started. I say this to say…a reason attendance is low is because we can't sit anymore…because He is doing heart surgery. And some of us were not ready.

I repeat—everyone wants revival until it gets messy. By that I mean it gets really uncomfortable when God goes into the areas of our lives that we didn't even know God had an issue with. This is the side of revival not many people talk about, but it is the product of revival. God doesn't put His finger on areas of our lives simply to condemn us—rather it's to make us more like His Son Jesus. He wants us to deal and remove those issues so we can be better conduits and hosts of His presence—that is what revival is all about… not the healings, good feelings, the emotional highs, or the physical manifestations, but being more like Jesus.

The next sentence may shock you but it can withstand scrutiny. Are you ready? Here it is. The level of glory a church experiences is not solely determined by a sovereign act of God but by the people within the local church. No one would disagree that God desires greater glory to manifest in all of our lives and churches; but we, His people, decide the amount of glory we want to oversee—it is our choice.

In other words, God will put all the glory on your church that it can and/or chooses to carry. This simply means, if the church members cannot or choose not to come alongside the pastors and help carry the glory of God, then the Lord will not send or increase the glory on the church. Shockingly, we can limit God and what He desires to be done. It happened with Israel:

*Yes, again and again they tempted God, and **limited** the Holy One of Israel* (Psalm 78:41).

Let me say it this way. If people pull away from participating and partnering with their leaders in the midst of a divine visitation, or if our schedules and personal agendas become more important than shouldering a revival, God will begin to lighten the load and will lessen the level of glory. This is a sobering fact of hosting His presence. He will reluctantly let us have our way.

This is why I constantly ask God to send us reinforcements and replacements because carrying God's glory is wonderful but difficult, and faithful people can get weary while others get distracted, discouraged, even offended, and some simply drop out.

God's glory is not cheap and He doesn't disburse it loosely. He waits until the conditions are right. We have the assurance that God will continue to pour out His glory and even increase it if the culture and environment can handle the weight.

30

I WANTED TO THROAT-PUNCH THE GUY

"The first step is a deep repentance, a breaking down of heart, getting down into the dust before God, with deep humility, and a forsaking of sin."
—CHARLES G. FINNEY

Have you ever made a declaration to God in the form of a promise and then kind of wished you hadn't? Well I did. It was a sincere declaration and I meant it with all my heart; however, I didn't know He was going to cash in on it in a matter of three seconds.

The revival was two months old; it was midmorning and I was at the altar in a time of extreme brokenness and hunger for more of God.

In front of our pulpit area there is a wooden altar bench about three feet wide. I remember kneeling in front of it one afternoon. Once again the sanctuary was dark and I was all alone spending time with God. Overwhelmed and astounded by His presence at our church, I boldly proclaimed to Him, "God, I love You so much and I will do whatever You ask and pay whatever price You want me to pay to have You here."

This sounds good, right? It is noble and inspiring, correct? But then He spoke. He interrupted the silence. I wasn't prepared for what He said, "Todd, you have hurt some people in your past, your previous elders, I need you to go make that right with them."

I froze in place.

Then I said as if I misunderstood His request, "Excuse me, God, what did You say?"

You see, I wasn't expecting that response at all; it caught me completely off guard. I simply went to the sanctuary to pray because I wanted more of Him, that's it.

God said again, "You hurt some people and I need you to go make that right."

I softly responded to the Lord as if He didn't have all the information necessary to make such a request. "God, they hurt me. They need to come to me and ask me to forgive them."

As soon as those words left my mouth I literally felt the Lord step away from me. He didn't leave me, but He simply pulled back. I felt it and knew He distanced Himself from me. It startled me.

Not that I need to remind you, but a few seconds earlier I made the boldest of proclamations, "Lord, I will do anything You ask and pay whatever price You want me to pay to have You and Your glory here at our church."

He and I both discovered at that precise moment the level of glory I could handle and carry. It was revealed to me that if I wasn't willing to obey Him, then I was at my limit. I had reached my capacity and He wasn't going to send more glory than we had already received.

After feeling the Lord withdraw, I promptly and brokenly agreed with the Lord that I would ask for forgiveness from the ones He would show me. I knew it was going to be an excruciating, painful, and humbling experience.

To make things more interesting, it had been many years since I had seen some of my previous elders. However, the moment I committed to make things right with them, they started crossing my path.

Going to these men and asking them to forgive me was one of the most difficult things I ever had to do. Every time I would see one of them the Lord would say, "There is one." My stomach would immediately get knotted up. I would begin to make excuses or say, "God, can I do it next time?"

One night I was enjoying dinner with my family and one of them walked into the restaurant. He had placed a to-go order and picked it up. And you guessed it, he made his way straight toward our table. I couldn't believe it. I said to myself, *You have got to be kidding me!* The Lord said, "There he is. I brought him to you."

I was trying not to make eye contact with him. Occasionally I looked up, hoping he would leave. The whole time he was talking I was having a conversation with myself and the Lord. I told the

Lord, "God, I'm eating dinner with my family and You know how important family time is. I can't do this now in front of everybody."

After a few minutes he said goodbye, and as he was headed out the door, the Lord said, "There he goes."

I said to the Lord, "I know, I know, but God...?" Deep down I knew God had brought him to me, not just in my vicinity, but exactly to my table. He was making it easy on me. My flesh didn't want to go and have the difficult conversation.

I glanced over at Karen, we made eye contact and I knew what I had to do. As he was exiting the restaurant, I got up from my chair and chased him down. I stopped him and said I needed him to forgive me. He was very gracious and God blessed our meeting. I felt God's peace come over me.

I must admit not every encounter went according to plan. One day I saw another elder in a parking lot. He and his wife were getting into their car, preparing to leave. The Lord said, "There he is."

I said, "I know, I see him." His car was parked about 200 yards from mine. Karen was with me and I told her I would be right back. She knew what I had to do. Those 200 yards felt like two miles. Every step of the way the devil was clowning with me, and my own mind was trying to convince me that I shouldn't do this, at least not now. But I was determined.

I finally made it to his car; he was standing outside the driver's door and his wife was in the passenger seat. After some short talk, I asked him to forgive me. Instead of saying, "Yes, I forgive you," he made a negative remark and then made a derogatory comment. This was unlike any other meeting I had had and it dazed me.

For a brief moment I wanted to throat-punch him right there in the parking lot. I took a deep breath and overcame my emotions by God's grace. The Lord calmed me down very quickly. I patiently listened to his concerns. Then I briefly ignored him and leaned into the car and spoke to his wife, asking her to forgive me as well. She had an altogether different response and it changed everything. I looked at him again and he softened and the two of us reconciled, it was beautiful.

Over a two-week period of time I satisfied the Lord's desire—and with each encounter I could sense the glory of God increasing in my life. The glory not only increased in my life but my church as a whole; our church services experienced a greater dimension of His presence.

Within a week I shared my experiences with my church. I felt they needed to know the journey I was on to walk softly and tenderly before the Lord.

I will never forget the overwhelming severity of the service. As I spoke about making things right with people whom we have hurt or offended, the fear and awe of the Lord came upon us. It was beautiful and dreadful at the same time. Because of God's loving care and conviction, the wonderful people at our church knew exactly what they had to do. Our desire was to please Him no matter the cost.

A Prodigal Returns Home

Jennifer, a single mom of three young men, felt the conviction of the Holy Spirit to make things right with someone in her past, her ex-best friend. Years earlier Jennifer's ex-best friend had an affair with her husband. He divorced Jennifer and married her best friend.

For years Jennifer hated them both. During the morning service when I shared my journey of forgiveness, while I was speaking the Lord convicted her that she needed to make things right by asking them to forgive her for hating them.

That afternoon she attended her son's birthday gathering. Everyone was there, including her ex-best friend and ex-husband. Jennifer interrupted the gathering and publicly asked her ex-husband and her ex-best friend to forgive her for hating them. They were shocked, but they forgave each other.

Her oldest son, Jordan, had been away from God; but that night at the North Georgia Revival, he fell under deep conviction and was gloriously set free in the baptismal waters. He had a dramatic encounter with Jesus in the water and has never been the same since.

Jennifer's brokenness and repentance to those she hated unlocked Heaven over her family. They were all touched and changed because of her obedience to the Lord.

A Foot Healed!

Kristy became part of a blended family when she was very young. Her biological mom was addicted to drugs, which had a devastating effect on her family. Her parents divorced and eventually her father married another woman. Kristy continued to live with her mom, making her childhood unpredictable and rough.

For example, when she was fifteen years old, her house was raided by the police. They entered the house and a policeman immediately threw her to the ground and pointed a gun at her head and commanded her not to move. She was handcuffed and questioned.

She wondered what was happening and why the police were in her home. Her mom and her mom's boyfriend were taken into custody—that's when Kristy discovered her mom was a drug dealer. Instantly her world was turned upside down.

As a result, Kristy was sent to live with her dad and his new wife. The transition was problematic from the start. She felt neglected, mistreated, unwanted, and even abandoned. In this new environment, even though she was living with her dad, she felt unprotected and it affected her relationship with her step-mom to an extreme measure.

Kristy had so much anger and resentment toward the two of them that at the age of sixteen she left home and moved in with a friend. Kristy describes her heart toward her stepmom, "I lived most of my life bitter and angry and had not forgiven her."

Fast-forward many years. One night while at home Kristy was watching the North Georgia Revival on Facebook. Her stepmother was entering the waters to be baptized. She said, "Something came over me and I was brought to tears." She added, "God allowed me to see my stepmom as His daughter, a good person who has struggles just like me." The Lord tenderly ministered to Kristy as her stepmother was encountering Jesus in the water.

The next week Kristy was at the North Georgia Revival, it was her first time and God laid it upon her heart to reconcile the relationship by asking her stepmother to forgive her. Kristy was taken back a little because she felt her stepmom first needed to apologize to her. But God was relentless and continued to press upon her.

That night Kristy decided to be baptized in the fire water; however, she didn't want to be baptized alone, she searched for her stepmother at the revival. She eventually found her and asked if both of them could be baptized together. Her stepmom agreed. I watched as the two of them entered the water. When Pastor Marty asked Kristi why she was in the water, in front of everyone she repented for hating her stepmother. The presence and glory of God gloriously manifested as both women repented to each other. They were both immersed in the fire water and God miraculously restored their relationship.

The story doesn't end in the water. A life-changing miracle resulted in Kristy's obedience. Kristy's daughter was born with an extra bone in her foot and it caused pain, extreme tightness, and it significantly restricted her mobility. For ten years she was closely monitored by the doctor and surgery was scheduled to remove the bone.

The Tuesday following their baptism, at a special children's ministry event hosted at our church, an altar call was given and her daughter came to the altar for prayer. Almost a dozen children gathered around her to pray for her foot. Within minutes, the Lord healed her and miraculously removed the extra bone. After prayer she got up and started running around the room without pain and with no limp.

Later that week she had a doctor's appointment; she told the doctor what happened at that special service. He instructed her to jump and run in the office, and she did! He said, "Do you feel any pain?" She said with a smile, "No!" The doctor was pleased and amazed. Oh by the way, the surgery was cancelled.

The power of forgiveness is enormous and the devil knows it. The enemy gives us a plethora of reasons why we shouldn't and cannot forgive others. But God's Word is very specific about this issue:

Matthew 5:23-24 (NIV): *"Therefore, if you are offering your gift at the altar and there remember that your brother or sister has something against you, leave your gift there in front of the altar. First go and be reconciled to them; then come offer your gift."*

Matthew 6:14-15 (NIV): *"For if you forgive other people when they sin against you, your heavenly Father will also forgive you. But if you do not forgive others their sins, your Father will not forgive your sins."*

Mark 11:25 (NIV): *"And when you stand praying, if you hold anything against anyone, forgive them, so that your Father in heaven may forgive you your sins."*

Colossians 3:13 (NIV): *"Bear with each other and forgive one another if any of you has a grievance against someone. Forgive as the Lord forgave you."*

The Scriptures reveal that unforgiveness and bitterness are the root causes of all types of ailments and delays in our lives. When we choose to not ask others to forgive us or even when we refuse to forgive others, the enemy has legal access, an open door to our lives. We literally give place to the devil. This is a high price to pay for an unwillingness to forgive or seek forgiveness.

Do a heart check and ask the Holy Spirit if there is anyone you need to forgive and/or ask to forgive you. When you obey His voice, Heaven will open over you and your family.

31

BOY HEALED WHEN DOCTOR FORGIVEN

"Faith sees the invisible, believes the unbelievable,
and receives the impossible."

—CORRIE TEN BOOM

His name is Isaac, a typical 13-year-old full of robust energy. However, one night when Katrina was pregnant with Isaac, she knew something wasn't right so she rushed to the emergency room. The hospital was overly crowded and the doctors were extremely busy. However, an ultrasound was ordered and revealed that Isaac's umbilical cord was wrapped around his neck.

Due to the high levels of amniotic fluid, Isaac was able to move around quite easily in Katrina's womb. As he moved around, because the cord was around his neck, his movements frequently cut off his oxygen supply. This caused stress on Isaac's developing brain, which resulted in more frantic movement.

Because of the high volume of patients in the emergency room, a doctor never attended to Katrina nor Isaac. Eventually the nurses sent them home after telling Katrina there was nothing they could do at this time.

Isaac's parents share what happened next.

> When Isaac was born it was immediately noticeable some things weren't normal. There was an immediate hush over the hospital room. I'll never forget that moment…I knew exactly what had happened and my 21-year-old self was overwhelmed with fear, anger, and guilt for not knowing better.
>
> There was damage to Isaac's brain.
>
> Throughout the years we have seen the best specialists and developmental pediatricians. There were abnormal MRIs. Five years after his birth, one of Isaac's neurologists found some white spots on his brain. She told us that it was most likely due to oxygen loss sometime during utero.
>
> The years that followed, Isaac has had significant struggles with learning. His "label" through the school system has been moderate to severe developmental delay. He loves books and loves to be read to and always wanted to learn to read. We have tried several programs, tutors, and private therapy with no success. We have even heard him cry out in his sleep, "I can't read."

Then, John and Carol Arnott, who led the great revival in Toronto called the Toronto Blessing, came and ministered at the North Georgia Revival. I, "Dad," was helping at the altar and watched as Pastor John asked people whose fault their ailments were and asked them to forgive those people. Over the next couple of days the Holy Spirit began to deal with my heart about unforgiveness for the doctors and nurses we saw during pregnancy. On Tuesday night of that week my wife and I prayed together and asked God to help us release the offense. We forgave them.

Wednesday we received a call from Isaac's teacher. She was crying talking about how Isaac's reading and school work had dramatically improved overnight. He was reading his books at school and adding numbers and even putting together fractions.

Remember, Isaac wasn't able to read anything even with tutoring, homeschooling for a season, private therapy, and after-school help. But today he continues to improve, including sentence structure, sensory processing, and overall academic improvement. It's a MIRACLE!

The breakthrough for Isaac came the night his parents chose to forgive the negligence of the doctors. Without question it had to be difficult, but they knew what God said about unforgiveness. Isaac benefited from their obedience.

There is no telling the miracles that are being held back over our lives, families, and churches due to unresolved conflict. I encourage you to investigate your heart, plus ask the Holy Spirit to search and reveal to you any offense you may have caused as well as the bitterness you may have toward others. Whatever He reveals, obey His desire. It will be worth it—it was for Isaac's parents!

32

YOU WILL BE EATEN
BY CANNIBALS

*"I have been bought with a price and I will live every
moment of this day so that the Great Purchaser of my
soul will receive the full reward of His suffering."*
—COUNT ZINZENDORF, The Moravian Brethren

In 1833, Charles Darwin, who introduced the theory of evolution, went to the South Sea Islands looking for the so-called "missing link." What he saw amazed him. When Darwin studied the islanders, he concluded there were no others more primitive and nothing on earth could lift them out of their state of being. He thought he found the lowliest of all mankind and that this people group would support his theory of evolution.

One of the obscure Christian heroes in the 19th century was John G. Paton (1824-1907). Interesting enough, Charles Spurgeon called Paton "The King of the Cannibals."

After serving for ten years as an urban missionary in Scotland, Paton began to feel the call of God on his life to reach an unreached people group in the New Hebrides, a small cluster of eight islands in the South Pacific Ocean between Hawaii and Australia. This is the same people group that Darwin called primitive and said, "...nothing on earth could lift them out of their state of being."

The people Paton desired to reach with the gospel were some of the most savage people on the planet. They were naked wild men who had a taste for blood.

For example, prior to Paton's arrival, two missionaries, John Williams and James Harris from the London Mission Society, attempted to evangelize the barbaric islanders. They made their way to the island of Erromanga on November 9, 1839, and both were killed shortly after making landfall, and shockingly were eaten by the cannibals they were trying to win to Jesus.

John Paton later wrote, "Thus were the New Hebrides baptized with the blood of martyrs; and Christ thereby told the whole Christian world that He claimed these islands as His own. His cross must yet be lifted up, where the blood of His saints has been poured forth in His name."[1]

Notoriously, it was the custom of the vicious and cruel natives to kill and then eat the flesh of their defeated enemies. Paton's friends who knew he was headed to the New Hebrides Islands found it difficult to give their support to his decision to minister to the people of the islands. Because of their love for John, many tried to dissuade him, one of his friends remarked, "The cannibals! You will be eaten by cannibals."

> John Paton responded, "Mr. Dickson, you are advanced in years now, and your own prospect is soon to be laid in the grave, there to be eaten by worms; I confess to you, that if I can live and die serving and honoring the Lord Jesus, it will make no difference to me whether I am eaten by Cannibals or by worms; and in the Great Day my resurrected body will arise far as yours in the likeness of our risen Redeemer."
>
> The old man left the room, exclaiming, "After that I have nothing more to say!"[2]

Paton, at the age of 32, left for the New Hebrides, and on November 5, 1958, his foot touched the island for the first time. He was enthusiastic to carry the message of Christ to the cannibals.

The ministry there was tough and within a few months after his arrival, his wife, Mary, gave birth to their son, Peter. His beloved wife died nineteen days later with typhoid fever. And just over a month later the newborn child died as well. John, with a broken heart, dug their graves with his bare hands and buried them in unmarked graves by the house he built.[3] He knew if he marked their graves the cannibals would dig them up and eat their bodies.

John's life was threatened often by the natives of which he said, "It is the sober truth that I had my nearest and most intimate glimpses of the presence of my Lord in those dread moments when musket, club or spear was being leveled at my life."[4]

But John Paton kept moving forward and didn't relent in his pursuit to make Christ known to the New Hebrides Islands. He married a lovely lady named Maggie and the two of them had ten children—four died early in life.

Paton never gave up and was able to raise money in order to purchase a steamboat that would take the gospel to the various islands. Over time he was able to write down the strange language of the islanders and create an alphabet. His hard work paid off; he eventually translated the Bible into their language.

John Paton's unwavering commitment to make Jesus known to the superstitious islanders was successful. His ministry covered twenty-five of the thirty small islands of New Hebrides. In 1858 the entire people group were cannibals and not a single Christian among them, but when John Paton died in January 28, 1907, it was reported the people were mostly all Christians and none were cannibals.

Thirty-four years later, Charles Darwin traveled back to the New Hebrides Islands on his ship, the HMS Beagle. He was amazed to see the islanders clothed and to see the school buildings, homes, and churches.[5] Obviously Darwin didn't believe in God, but if he did it would have been because of what he saw as a result of John G. Paton's preaching the gospel to the inhabitants of the New Hebrides Islands. Darwin later said, "The march of improvement, consequent on the introduction of Christianity throughout the South Sea, probably stands by itself in the records of history."[6] Charles was so moved by what he saw he gave a generous financial gift to London Missionary Society.

John G. Paton certainly fulfilled the Scripture in Revelation 12:11 (NIV), *"...they did not love their lives so much as to shrink from death."*

ENDNOTES

1. John G. Paton: *Missionary to the New Hebrides, An Autobiography* Edited by His Brother (Edinburgh: The Banner of Truth Trust, 1965, orig. 1889, 1891), 75.
2. John G. Paton, John G. Paton, D.D., *Missionary to the New Hebrides; An Autobiography* (London: Hodder and Stoughton, 1891), 56.
3. Woodrow Kroll, *Giants of the Old Testament: Lessons on Living From Moses* (Lincoln, NE: Back to the Bible), 22.
4. Missionary Short Biography, John Paton; https://www.youtube .com/watch?v=n-qq_JtJth4; accessed May 20, 2020.
5. Bruce Howell, "In 1833 Charles Darwin Went to the South Sea," Sermon Central; accessed May 20, 2020.
6. *Charles Darwin: The Voyage of the Beagle: Journal of Researches into the Natural History and Geology of the Countries Visited During the Voyage of the H.M.S. Beagle Round the World* (New York: Random House, 2001), 451.

33

DON'T LEAVE THE ICE

"Prayer turns ordinary mortals into men of power. It brings power. It brings fire. It brings rain. It brings life. It brings God."
—SAMUEL CHADWICK

In the early years of the fourth century, AD 320, on a frozen lake near Sevaste, Lesser Armenia (present-day Turkey), forty Roman soldiers of the elite and famous Thundering Legion declined the decree to bow their knees to Roman Emperor Licinius and the gods of Rome.

The soldiers of the Thundering Legion were the bravest and finest fighting men in the whole Roman army. They were arduously trained, highly skilled, and battle tested.

Emperor Licinius ruled the eastern half of the Roman Empire and had issues with the Christian contingent who lived there. He wanted to eradicate Christianity from the land under his rulership. In an attempt to do so, he thought he had to purge the Christians from his own ranks, so he ordered all Roman soldiers under his jurisdiction to recant their loyalty and worship of the Christian God. His decree—all soldiers must show their sole allegiance to him and the pagan gods of Rome.

The immediate commander of the Thundering Legion received his orders and questioned all to see if there were any Christians under his command. He asked, "Are any of you devout Christians?" To his surprise, forty of his strongest and best men stepped forward.

Right away the soldiers were instructed to demonstrate their dedication to the empire by burning incense, offering sacrifices, and bowing down to the idols that were put in front of them. All forty soldiers refused to obey the edict to worship the pagan gods.

Governor Agricola became aware of their rejection of the decree and addressed the group, "I am told you refuse to offer the sacrifice ordered by Emperor Licinius."

One of the soldiers spoke on behalf of the rest. "We will not sacrifice. To do so is to betray our holy faith."

Their commander tried to bribe the lone forty soldiers by promising money, high honors, and notoriety with the emperor if they would simply comply with the decree. The soldiers were steadfast and were unmoved by the lucrative offers.

The forty soldiers who refused to cooperate with the decree were forthrightly stripped of their military rank. In addition, they were forced to remove their clothing and were publicly humiliated by being dragged out into the cold, flogged, and brutally tortured. Afterward they were placed in a dark, frigid prison cell. Beaten, torn, and bleeding, not one of the forty recanted their faith. Together they stood firm and refused to bow down before the rogue gods of the empire.

With continued respectful defiance, the soldiers were anchored to their commitment to honor Jesus—even if it meant dying for their Savior. The patience of the Roman hierarchy was waning. Again, elaborate gifts were offered to the soldiers if they would simply comply with the harmless edict from Emperor Licinius. They were resolute in their resolve and once again refused all bribes.

The Roman leaders were left with no other choice; this rebellion within the ranks had to be crushed. Therefore, an order was given to take the forty men to the frozen pond. Commander Lysias said, "You will stand naked on the ice until you agree to sacrifice to the gods."

The winter had been brutal and excessively cold. The leaders thought for sure this form of torture would cause them to recant their faith and return to the fighting ranks. They were wrong. As the forty marched toward the frozen pond, one soldier shouted, "We are soldiers of the Lord and fear no hardship." Another one yelled, "What is our death but entrance into eternal life?"

The order was clear—strip them naked and expose their bodies to the arctic air. By all accounts this was a cruel and barbaric form of punishment. It would be a slow and torturous way to die.

The report was that many of these soldiers voluntarily took their clothes off and willingly marched to the center of the ice-covered pond counting themselves fortunate and worthy to suffer for Christ.

As they stood on the ice, they clung together both physically and spiritually. Throughout the night they encouraged each other to persevere and to suffer courageously until the very end. They didn't want to relinquish their loyalty to Jesus.

According to the record, this was the soldiers' joint prayer: "Lord, there are forty of us engaged in this battle; grant that forty may be crowned and not one be missing from this sacred number."

As a matter of mental torture and enticement, the governor gave the command to make fires on the bank of the pond and to have baths filled with warm water and placed at the edge of the pond. This cruel gesture was meant to tempt and lure many of the soldiers off the ice.

Huddled together in the middle of the pond, the forty soldiers prayed, "God has ordained it for us to be brothers in this life. Let us pray that we may have the strength to be brothers unto eternity. And we pray oh Lord that this sacred number of the forty of us will not be broken and that each of us earn our crowns tonight."

There they stood firm with their bare feet on top of the blood-stained ice, shivering. Sadly, some of the soldiers could hang on no longer and perished. Unfortunately, in the middle of the night as well, the lure of the steam from the baths on the bank and the adjacent fires, one of the soldiers could not persevere and succumbed to the cold and the temptation for warmth. As he left the group and walked away, the others encouraged him to turn back and not leave the ice but to stay faithful and to hang on to the end.

He didn't listen to the shivering echoes from his remaining friends on the ice, but instead made his way to the shore. Immediately he was celebrated and escorted into one of the warm tubs of water. The influx of heat from the water so shocked his frozen system that it sent him into convulsions and he died a horrible death.

The others were disappointed and heartbroken for their comrade, but the morale of the soldiers remained high. They knew it wouldn't be much longer until they, one by one, would pass over into eternity and at last gaze into the eyes of the One they so diligently loved, Jesus.

One of the guards, Aglaius, earlier in the night while the forty soldiers were standing naked on the ice had a vision. He saw heavenly powers, like angels distributing crowns on the heads of the forty soldiers. This alarmed and shook him to the very core of his soul. He reconciled that what was happening on the ice with these forty men was genuine. Furthermore, he was shocked and amazed that these men were willing to pay the ultimate price to demonstrate their loyalty for Jesus.

When the one defector left the group and died on the shore, Aglaius stripped off his armor and clothes, threw his helmet to the ground, proclaimed himself a Christian and ran onto the ice to join the others making their number forty once again.

When the sun arose in the east, all forty men lay motionless on the ice. All of them had died or were close to death. The order was given to gather the bodies and place them on a cart. The soldiers were then instructed to burn them and throw their ashes and bones into the river so to be forgotten.

These forty soldiers died with their faith fully intact. They finished their race well and fully embodied Revelation 12:11, "And they overcame him by the blood of the Lamb and by the word of their testimony, and they did not love their lives to the death."

These soldiers were real people, many of them were married and had small children back home. All had mothers and fathers, some of them were the younger brother of the family, each with a life to live. But they so loved Him; they chose to give up their lives to their glorious Savior rather than bow their knee to a pagan god.

May we not forget these martyrs. Here are their names, take a prayerful look:

Acacius, Aetius, Aglaius, Alexander, Angus, Athanasius,

Candidus, Chudion, Claudius, Cyril, Cyrion, Dometian, Domnus, Ecdicus, Elias, Eunoicus, Eutyches, Eutychius, Flavius, Gaisus, Gorgonius, Helianus, Heraclius, Hesychius, John, Lysimachus, Meliton, Nicholas, Pholoctemon, Priscus, Sacerdon, Servian, Sisinus, Smaragdus, Theodulus, Theophilus, Valens, Valerius, Vivanus, and Zanthias. [1]

I believe that today these forty are around God's throne singing His praises and are part of the great company of witnesses in Hebrews 11 who are watching the advancement of the Church. May their ultimate sacrifice not be in vain and squandered by an entitled and fickle Church. And rightfully so, may our devotion to our King be any less.

Paul says,

> *According to my earnest expectation and hope that in nothing I shall be ashamed, but with all boldness, as always, so now also Christ will be magnified in my body, whether by life or by death. For to me, to live is Christ, and to die is gain* (Philippians 1:20-21).

If at any time in history we need Christians like the forty martyrs of Sevaste it is now. The world must see the manifestation of genuine faith that is fleshed out in power fueled by a raw relentless love for Jesus.

Keep fighting. Stay true. Remain faithful. Don't give in to temptation and the seduction of fainting pleasures. The warm waters are appealing in the cold seasons of your life, but press on. If all your family and friends leave the ice, you must not. Be the one who finishes the race.

The echo from the forty, "Don't leave the ice!"

ENDNOTE

1. This event has been paraphrased from the following two sources: "40 Martyrs of Sevaste," Christianity.com; https://www .christianity.com/church/church-history/timeline/301-600/40 -martyrs-of -sevaste-11629648.html; accessed May 20, 2020. "In Memory of the Forty Martyrs of Sebaste—A.D. 320"; http:// fortymartyrs.org/Forty-Martyrs-of-Sebaste.html; accessed May 20, 2020.

34

IT WILL COST YOU EVERYTHING

"Go home. Lock yourself in a room. Kneel down in the middle of the floor and with a piece of chalk, draw a circle around yourself. There, on your knees, pray fervently and brokenly, that God would start a revival within that chalk circle."
—Gypsy Smith

John Knox is probably best known for his prayer "Give me Scotland, or I die." He had such a love for Jesus and his fellow countrymen that he was willing to do whatever it took to see them saved. This wasn't an emotional plea, his words were not weightless, but a passionate prayer that revealed he counted the cost and was willing to pay the ultimate price for the cause of Christ.

In these disturbing times we need men, women, teenagers, and children who have the same ferocious spirit as John Knox who passionately cry out, "Give me revival, or I die!" Even as I write this I sense a deep hunger arising across the land. There is a holy disturbance taking place in the hearts of God's people.

Like Moses, who knew if he saw the face of God he would die, it didn't matter—his quest for God and His glory was worth the risk. In essence he said, "Even if it kills me, show me Your glory!"

Recently I cried out for God to increase His glory in my life. He immediately responded, "Increase your brokenness." He was letting me know that there is no shortcut to the glory of God. It comes with a high price. I have learned a hard lesson—the level of glory in my life is directly proportionate to my level of brokenness.

Kathryn Kuhlman (1907-1976) was a powerful woman of God who traveled the world sharing Christ and demonstrated an amazing healing ministry. She preached an uncompromising gospel and demonstrated the power of the Kingdom as many blind, crippled, deaf, and diseased were dramatically healed. Unprecedented miracles occurred in her crusades. In one of her messages in front of thousands of people, she revealed the price she had to pay to have such a powerful healing ministry. Here are her words:

> It costs everything. If you really want to know the price, it will cost you everything. Kathryn Kuhlman died a long time ago. I know the day, I know the hour. I can go to the spot where Kathryn Kuhlman died. For me it was easy because I had nothing. I know better than anyone else from whence I come, a little cross-road town in Missouri, a population of 1,200 people. I had nothing. I was born

without talent. Most people are born with something. I didn't even have hair on my head when I was born, just red fuzz. One day I just looked up and said, "Wonderful Jesus I have nothing. I have nothing to give you but my love. That's all I can give you. And I love you with all my heart. I give you my body, a living sacrifice. If you can take nothing and use it, then here is nothing. Take it." It isn't silver vessels He is asking for; it isn't golden vessels that He needs. He just needs yielded vessels.[1]

Kuhlman also said it takes tremendous sacrifice: "Its terms require a surrender which the average Christian is unwilling to make. Things that are gotten cheap are usually cheap. The things you have to pay most for are usually the things that are most valuable."

The great missionary Hudson Taylor, who founded the China Inland Mission, knew exactly what it would cost to win that dark communist country to Christ: "China is not to be won for Christ by quiet, ease-loving men and women…The stamp of men and women we need is such as will put Jesus, China, [and] souls first and foremost in everything and at every time—even life itself must be secondary."[2]

This level of commitment is one the common denominators behind every move of God.

Count Zinzendorf of the Moravian Brethren said, "I have been bought with a price. And I will live every moment of this day so that the Great Purchaser of my soul will receive the full reward of His suffering."

William Booth, founder of the Salvation Army may have captured the key to it all, "The greatness of a man's power is the measure of his surrender."

Surrender, death, and sacrifice are words not commonly used in pulpits today; however, things are changing. Pastors and leaders are becoming aware of the fact that our well-thought plans and cutely organized sermon series are failing us—we are realizing we need more, much more.

Oswald J. Smith, who was a Canadian pastor and author said, "I have seen the vision and for self I cannot live. Life is less than worthless till my all I give."

Think long and hard about what is being said by these giants of the faith; look at their level of sacrifice and self-denial. They reveal to us the secret of their success. God wants to send His power and glory to every believer, but He will not until individuals come to the end of themselves.

Robert Jaffray was a brilliant man as well as a great preacher. He was a missionary to China and founded the first Chinese missionary society called the "Chinese Foreign Missionary Union." He was persecuted and endured much opposition. However, because of his faith and love for the people of that region of the world, the last three years of his life were spent in a Japanese internment camp. He died in 1945 from illness and malnutrition. For many this was a tragic end to such a wonderful Christian life, but Jaffray was pleased to prove his love for Jesus.

What many people didn't know was that Jaffray was also heir to Canada's largest newspaper based in Toronto, the *Globe and Mail*. As a young man he felt a call of God to be a missionary, and God laid on his heart the beautiful people of China. As soon as possible he started studying the Chinese language.

At the same time, the Standard Oil Company knew he was an extraordinarily bright young man and wanted to hire him. They desperately wanted his services and offered him a huge salary. He graciously turned them down. The Standard Oil Company responded a little later, "We have doubled the offer." He again said, "No." Then they sent a one-line telegram which said, "Jaffray, at any price." He wrote back with one line as well, "Your salary is big, your job is too small."

It's all about perspective, isn't it? You and I get to choose how we are going to live our lives. We decide how much we sacrifice for Him. My desire is that Galatians 2:20 becomes our current reality, *"I have been crucified with Christ; it is no longer I who live, but Christ lives in me; and the life which I now live in the flesh I live by faith in the Son of God, who loved me and gave Himself for me."*

Paul better than anyone understood that our human flesh is incredibly influential and filled with unhealthy passions and desires. He said, *"Those who belong to Christ have crucified the flesh with its passions and desires"* (Galatians 5:24 NIV). This crucifixion is and should be self-imposed. We all know crucifixion is torturous, painful, and quite frankly, not pleasant. The staple prayer of Evans Roberts and the people of Wales who experienced the Welsh revival in 1904 was, "Bend the Church and save the world."

It is this level of abandonment that attracts the glory of God to humanity. Nothing short of full, unequivocal surrender and denial. A.B. Simpson summed it up best, "We must surrender ourselves so utterly that we can never own ourselves again. We must hand over self and all its rights in an eternal covenant and give God the absolute right to own us, control us and possess us forever."

C.T. Studd said, "If Jesus Christ be God, and died for me, then no sacrifice can be too great for me to make for Him."

I am reminded of a story I discovered about a pastor in India. Before his conversion he was a staunch atheist and aggressive communist. The Lord one night appeared to him in a dream and shortly after was dramatically saved. Currently, six thousand wonderful churches have been planted. He has done this in a land where tens of thousands of Christians have been martyred and to this day thousands are losing their lives every year. He has an interesting approach to his baptismal ceremony. He asks each new convert one question: "Are you willing to follow Jesus to your last breath, to your last drop of blood?"

This same question must be echoed from the pulpits around the world. Our commitment to Jesus must and should require us to give our all to Him even if it means laying down our lives.

I think we need to take a hard look at what theologian Douglas Wilson said,

> A great reformation and revival—it will happen the same way the early Christians conquered Rome. Their program of conquest consisted largely of two elements: gospel preaching and being eaten by lions, a strategy that has not yet captured the imagination of the contemporary church.

ENDNOTES

1. Kathryn Kuhlman, "It Will Cost You Everything"; https://www
    .youtube.com/watch?v=wkuvXqVz-xc; accessed May 21, 2020.
2. "Hudson Taylor," Christianity Today; https://www
    .christianitytoday.com/history/people/missionaries/hudson
    -taylor.html; accessed May 21, 2020.

ABOUT THE AUTHOR

Todd Smith and his wife, Karen, have served as the senior pastors of Christ Fellowship Church since 2009. Along with serving in pastoring roles for more than twenty-five years, he has preached the Gospel, led crusades, traveled to the missions fields, and participated in pastors conferences in more than twenty-five countries around the world. He has also planted five churches in the United States.

Pastor Todd has authored six books: *40 Days; I Found the Secret; Word Power; He Sat Down; He Sent Him* and *Speaking In Tongues: Your Secret Weapon.* He earned a Bachelor of Science degree from Samford University in Birmingham, Alabama, a Master of Divinity from Southwestern Baptist Theological Seminary, and a Doctor of Ministry from Faith Theological Seminary.

In his spare time Todd loves spending time with his boys, Ty and Ebo, hunting, and pulling hard for the Alabama Crimson Tide! Pastor Todd and Karen are currently traveling all across the nation and worldwide spreading revival fire wherever they minister.